George Smith Drew

Nazareth: Its life and lessons

Second Edition

George Smith Drew

Nazareth: Its life and lessons
Second Edition

ISBN/EAN: 9783337257781

Printed in Europe, USA, Canada, Australia, Japan

Cover: Foto ©Lupo / pixelio.de

More available books at **www.hansebooks.com**

NAZARETH.

BY THE SAME AUTHOR,

THE DIVINE KINGDOM ON EARTH AS IT IS IN HEAVEN.

Demy 8vo. cloth, 10s. 6d.

'Our COMMONWEALTH is in Heaven.'

'No one can rise from the study of this book without riper and larger ideas of the designs and purposes of the Divine mind in the constitution of His Church.—*English Churchman.*

NAZARETH:

ITS LIFE AND LESSONS.

BY

G. S. DREW, M.A.

VICAR OF HOLY TRINITY, LAMBETH;
AUTHOR OF 'SCRIPTURE LANDS,' 'REASONS OF FAITH,' &c.

'In Him was Life, and the Life was the Light of men.'

SECOND EDITION.

HENRY S. KING & CO.
65 CORNHILL & 12 PATERNOSTER ROW, LONDON.
1873.

ll rights reserved)

PREFACE.

THE following pages contain an expansion, in some detail, of the introductory paragraphs of Chapter V. of the 'Divine Kingdom on Earth as it is in Heaven.' In that part of the book the writer dwelt upon Christ's Human Life as the typal embodiment of the Divine Order of Existence, and here he has endeavoured to enlarge his observations on its earlier years, in that view of them. In carrying out this purpose, he has made careful use of the chief authorities which have informed us respecting the period under consideration, as well as of his own recollections of Nazareth and its neighbourhood, where the work which he has now attempted to execute, was meditated, many years ago, while he was passing amidst the scenes which he describes.

With these helps in endeavouring to transfer himself to the place and period in which the earlier years of Christ's course were passed, and using them under the conviction that a true Human, as well as Divine Life, was then lived by Him, the writer believes that he has brought out some results of an importance which is sufficient to claim for them the attention of thoughtful and devout readers. He might have produced a much larger, and perhaps a more popularly attractive work, if he had permitted himself to indulge any exercise of mere imagination in connection with his subject; but he felt that he was warned off from every indulgence of this kind, by the very significant reserve of the Evangelists, as well as by the excesses, in that direction, of those 'despicable monuments of religious fiction' which are known as the Apocryphal Gospels. He has, in fact, simply confined himself to setting forth the outlines of our Lord's Life throughout those thirty years, *such as we know it must have been* when we bear in mind the Design of His Incarnation, and the results of the earlier which are witnessed in the later stages of His ministry amongst mankind. And of set purpose, he has left these outlines to be filled up by the careful meditations of his readers.

It is with unfeigned diffidence that he refers to these words, 'such as we know the Life must have been,' when he remembers how invariably commentators on the Gospel History speak of this portion of the Redeemer's course as marked by 'absolute obscurity,' and as having been 'studiously withdrawn from human knowledge.' Long-continued thought upon the subject, however, emboldens him to ask, Is this often repeated, and generally accepted, dictum indeed well-founded? Why should the reserve of the Evangelists be regarded as tantamount to the prohibition of enquiry in this instance, when it is not so regarded with respect to many occasions in the later period of Christ's ministry, where interpreters do not hesitate to fill up and illuminate, from extraneous sources, that which has been only briefly set forth in the Inspired Record? Facts which illustrate the period in question are within our reach, and we have not been forbidden to ascertain and examine them. Now this being the case, ought not those facts to receive due consideration, and indeed is not attention to them necessary in order to complete our view of Christ's fulfilment of the mission for which He came into the world?

He came to live a Life which should be the 'Light of men.' In other words, the Design of His Incarnation was to embody, and by embodying to reflect, and so openly reveal, the Divine form and order of man's existence. Surely this is the true view and statement of the Purpose of the Eternal Word, rather than that which speaks of 'plans' formed by Him at the outset of His course, and of far-sighted methods which He then devised for their after execution. The object of His earthly ministry was the fulfilment—not of any freshly formed scheme, but —of the Eternal Purpose and Design of God, that fulfilment being carried forward amidst the circumstances, the duties and relationships, of an ordinary life. And this being so, is not the distinct recognition of that larger portion of His course, wherein indeed we see the greater part of the majority of human lives reflected, absolutely necessary? One can hardly imagine any other than a simply assenting answer to this question. But such an assent gives an ample justification to the apparently presumptuous attempt on which the writer has ventured in these pages.

Their simple purpose is to remove, with fitting care and reverence, that veil of reserve which has been so wisely[1] drawn over this as over many later portions of the Life (*where a similar removal is attempted by every com-*

---

[1] See Introduction, *infra*, p. 5.

mentator on the Gospel History), so that, as nearly as possible, we too may see our Lord as He was actually seen by those who 'companied with Him' in the earlier days of His mortality. *He was not hidden from them during that period, in any mysterious retirement. And why, then, is it necessary that He should be so hidden from ourselves?* This question deserves to be well pondered. And here, too, we may remark, as a further incitement to careful diligence in making the attempt which it has suggested, that far more than the complete vision of a true human life will be obtained if the work is, in any measure, successfully effected. For in that vision we shall see manifested the unity of the Divine Order of the universe: its 'continuity and its correlations' will be unfolded. In the book above referred to, the present writer has endeavoured to bring some tokens of that unity of our existence into view. For many years he has striven to do this, under the ever-strengthening conviction that the vision of this, unity, of the harmoniously blended connections of our earthly with our heavenly existence, will be more helpful than any other means can prove, in clearing up perplexities by which Christian men are sorely troubled at this time, as well as in removing some of the causes of their too well founded apprehensions as to the 'things which are coming upon the earth.'

Moreover, there are many practical uses, in life as well as thought, that may be made of the enquiries and contemplations which are here brought forward. Some of them are hinted at in the closing chapter, as well as in the Appendix, where the writer has ventured to reproduce some reflections, published by him more than twenty-five years ago, which bear upon the subject. They are commended to the livers of 'dreary lives,' to toilers and workers in hidden places, in the strong belief that such persons may be greatly helped, in their 'times of need,' by seeing in the 'Life at Nazareth' a frequent reflection of their own, in its saddened weariness, and its consequent temptations to restlessness and discontent.

January 1872.

NOTE.—*Some of the practical lessons above referred to, are urged with much wisdom and tenderness in the (just published) 'Home Life of Jesus of Nazareth,' by the Rev. A. Gurney. The book in the reader's hands was printed, and almost ready for publication, before Mr. Gurney's work appeared, or the writer would gladly have referred to it in Chap. II., on the 'Home and Family Life in Nazareth,' and in the 'Concluding Application.'*

CONTENTS.

CHAPTER		PAGE
	INTRODUCTION	1
I.	INFANCY AND EARLY CHILDHOOD IN NAZARETH	17
II.	HOME AND FAMILY LIFE IN NAZARETH	35
III.	LIFE IN THE NAZARETH COMMUNITY	53
IV.	NAZARETH LIFE IN THE NATION	72
V.	CHURCH LIFE IN NAZARETH	88
VI.	NAZARETH LIFE IN ITS AFTER DEVELOPMENTS	105
VII.	CONCLUDING APPLICATION	119

APPENDIX.

NOTE A.	*Reasons for the Silence of the Evangelists respecting the Events of the Thirty Years*	131
NOTE B.	*Nazareth and its Neighbourhood*	133
NOTE C.	*On Jesus increasing in Wisdom*	137
NOTE D.	*On the Synagogue and its Worship*	139
NOTE E.	*Practical Lessons*	141

They returned into Galilee, to their own city Nazareth. And the child grew, and waxed strong in spirit, filled with wisdom, and the grace of God was upon Him.—St. LUKE.

In all things it behoved Him to be made like unto his brethren, that He might be a merciful and faithful High Priest. —Ep. to HEB.

The Life was manifested, and we have seen it, and bear witness, and shew unto you that eternal Life which was with the Father, and was manifested unto us.—St. JOHN.

NAZARETH:

ITS LIFE AND LESSONS.

INTRODUCTION.

OUR knowledge of God, and of our place and relations in His kingdom, has been mainly derived from Revelation. Those facts of our position which man could not ascertain by his unaided powers, have been made known by means of special agencies divinely appointed for this end. For the purpose, however, of guarding against an unseemly exposure of heavenly verities, and in order to quicken devout and thoughtful minds in their researches, the Revealer has always observed what may well be called a wise frugality in His communications. And man's own researches and meditations have been required to fill out, and illuminate, many of the disclosures which have been thus authentically conveyed to him.

Luke ii. 19, 51.

Butler's Analogy, pt. ii. ch. iii.

While, accordingly, he has thoughtfully dwelt on these disclosures, and trustfully 'pondered them in his heart,' the meaning of revealed facts and principles has been enlarged within his view: the divine communications have grown more living and significant. It was thus with the oral revelation which God made in the earliest ages to His servants, and with the truths that have been conveyed by the ordinances which He instituted. While, in all essential respects, the meaning of those communications was apprehended by seers and prophets from the first, it was ever enlarging and deepening in their consciousness. They gradually perceived verities which were involved in the connections of the inspired statements, and in the inferences which flowed from them. This has also been the case with respect to the knowledge which is conveyed by Holy Scripture. Minds well informed by history and science, and quickened also by newly arisen needs, have 'compared and pursued intimations,' scattered up and down the inspired pages, which had been 'overlooked by the generality of the world'; they have 'traced out obscure hints dropped, as if accidentally, or which seemed to come into their minds by chance,' and have thus caused fresh aspects of the heavenly disclosures, and of the Divine Life, to be brought out continually with an impressiveness which has been altogether unexpected. Then again, the special needs of each age, and its thought-movements growing so often into the vagaries of heresy and the negations of unbelief, have further quickened this activity in the minds of saints and theologians who have thus been moved to look and enquire in directions that would otherwise have been neglected. The errors of men, as well as their most genuine efforts of thought and their sincerest aspirations, have thus, and often very remarkably, subserved and furthered an effective elucidation of the truth.

In this manner, and by all these agencies, enlarged views of the Divine Life and Kingdom have opened out in every direction. The Church's consciousness has widened and deepened, and it has been continually enriched. And everywhere the process is still being carried forward by means of learned research and of prayerful meditation; but in no instance has it proceeded with more successful earnestness than in the enquiries which are continually bringing out fresh aspects of Christ's Life and Character, and larger knowledge of the relations which He is sustaining towards

Margin: INTRODUCTION.
1 Cor. xi. 19.
Divine Kingdom, ch. vi.
Divine Kingdom. ubi sup.

mankind. Very naturally men's thoughts have ever turned hitherward with most interest, and it is to an important but comparatively neglected view of this subject that our attention is here directed.

We are referring to that large portion of His earthly course which was passed, almost unobserved, and in comparative seclusion and secrecy, at Nazareth. Through those many years he lived on continuously, day after day, an actual human life; gradually 'waxing strong in spirit, and increasing in wisdom,' while He discharged the duties and filled out the relationships that belonged to the position which He had chosen. Now the course which He pursued through all those years, formed part of that Life which has been declared to be the 'Light of men.' Then, too, as well as afterwards, we must recognise Him as the Eternal Word, through Whom the mind and will of God have been communicated to His creatures—unless indeed we are, however unconsciously, entertaining the heresies which affirm that His Divine and Human natures were first united at His Baptism. Part of His Revealing Work must have then been going forward; and surely from that part also information and instruction may be derived. Indeed we should reverse conclusions that have ever been

[margin: INTRODUCTION.]
[margin: Luke ii. 40, 52.]
[margin: John i. 4. viii. 12.]
[margin: Neander's Church History.]

accepted by the Church, and negative the first principles of Catholic Belief, if we questioned the assertion that His conduct and His words, His abstinences and His activities, were as significant then as they were afterwards. Nor can it be doubted that the meaning which was conveyed by them was intended for man's use, and for the promotion of His welfare and advancement.

It is true, indeed, that very little has been related respecting that part of His human course. Nay, it may even be acknowledged that, in some measure, it was intentionally veiled; and that, for this end, special influences were exerted upon the minds of the Evangelists. We can hardly doubt that, had they been left to themselves, they would have dilated, after the fashion of other biographers, on the circumstances of His childhood and youth, and on the general habits of His life before His public ministry began. Evidently they were led by an external and higher influence—the nature of which every Christian reader will devoutly recognise—to fence off, from the observation of hasty superficial gazers, this part of His course as man amongst mankind. Still, fully admitting the fact that, for these reasons, little has been said about those thirty years, we do not by any means regard

Appendix,
Note A.

> *(Introduction.)*
>
> *(Matthew xiii. 11.)*
>
> *(Luke ii. 19, 51.)*

it as equivalent to an admonition that we should abstain from all enquiry and thought respecting the manner of His life as they went forward. The reserve of the Evangelists is indeed remarkable, and it is of a nature which is well fitted to deter the enquiries of men who would not have been profited by what they looked upon, if this part of the Divine Life had been made fully known. Yet, as we shall see, their silence is not absolute. The veil which they have cast over Christ's abode in Nazareth is not impenetrable, or of such a nature that enquirers of earnest and devout temper need be hindered from an attempt to pierce through its obscurity. On the contrary, this part of the narrative invites the attention of those who are accustomed to 'ponder in their hearts'; in other words, to weigh, lovingly and trustfully as well as thoughtfully, every Divine communication. Men who look in such a spirit towards that Galilean town and its surroundings, and who have duly qualified themselves to estimate the import of the few but most significant words that have been written respecting the Life that was passed in it, who observe the subject under all the lights that converge upon that place and time—will find it marvellously illumined in their view. The Divine

Life which was lived and witnessed there, will come out with a clearness and definiteness which, until they thus applied themselves to look for it, could not have been imagined.

This is the effect, if the period of which we are speaking, is surveyed in the spirit and from the point of view, as well as with the helps, which have just been indicated. Then the same results will follow which, in so many other similar instances, have rewarded diligent enquiry, and devout and steadfast meditation. And here, in a few pages, we will point out three of the principal sources of information which, in this temper and spirit, should be used; naming as the first of them a heedful regard to the main Purposes of the Incarnation.

<small>Hosea vi. 3. *Divine Kingdom*, ubi sup.</small>

I. These Purposes may be securely learned when we carefully observe the scope of the Divine Communications, and investigate their substance. And being perceived, they cast invaluable light on the entire Gospel History, and, indeed, on all the supernatural dispensations. Nor is any part of those dispensations more effectively illuminated by these means than that to which we are now looking.— What, then, were these purposes, except to embody man's aboriginal nature in his view, and in that nature to reveal afresh the Divine Plan and Order

<small>John i. 4, 1 John i. 1, 2.</small>

of his life? Humanity, in its originally perfect reflection of God's Image, was, as in a second Adam, to be manifested again in Christ. Moreover, in this perfect form, He came to live through man's appointed course, thereby perfectly disclosing all the laws by which it is controlled. In His individual life, in His purely personal relations towards God and all His creatures, as well as in the discharge of every social obligation, He undertook to make known the rules of our true existence, and the manner in which we should fulfil our part of the Economy into which we have been brought. In other words, He came to show, both in His Person and His Life, what God had constituted man to be, and what, amidst all his duties and relationships, He meant him to become.

Micah vi. 8.

Now what is in fact the true form of human life, and what are the order and laws which should be observed in it, may be gathered from the injunctions of Holy Scripture, and from the examples and aspirations, nay, even from the condemned failures, of the men whose habits and proceedings, interpreted by heavenly wisdom, have been therein recorded. In the inspired pages, and especially in Christ's own teaching, interpreted and completed by that of His Apostles, we may see, with hardly any possibility of misapprehension, the perfect ideal of a human course; and any error or defect in our conception of it, may be corrected by the fuller details of His after life, when these are illustrated by the precepts and instructions of His disciples. From such sources the true and typal form of human being may be accurately learned; and we are sure that it was in that form His existence passed, as He lived through childhood and youth and early manhood, in His home and neighbourhood, in the nation and in the Church. When we bear this fact in mind we can at once ascertain the main distinctions of His conduct and demeanour as son and brother, as neighbour and friend and citizen, amidst the toils of life, in its sufferings and its enjoyments—while He lived on, day by day, and year after year, through the thirty years to which our attention is directed. The characteristic features of His path during that long period, the marked and prominent relationships into which He was brought by it, are, in this manner, unmistakably disclosed.

II. Then again, besides remembering in general that at that time His life was conformed to the true pattern of existence, and learning by this means the chief features that distinguished it,

marginal notes: INTRODUCTION. 1 John i. 2. John viii. 46.

we also know, definitely and in detail, the outward conditions amidst which it was carried forward. We have been told under what terms and in what framework, the ideal of existence was then embodied in His person. The direction and limits of His earthly course in Nazareth have been clearly indicated. We are familiar with the scene, and can observe the circumstances, the shape and costume, in which this Divine pattern of man's life was manifested through that period. Thus far the direct notices of the Evangelists respecting this early period of His career, brief as they are, and fragmentary, may be looked on, and especially when those notices are connected with the allusions to it afterwards, as furnishing definite information.

Unmistakably they point out the place in which He lived, the social position which He occupied, and the nature of the occupations in which the purposes of His Incarnation were then accomplished. We know the aspect of His abode and its surroundings. Its physical characteristics and conditions illustrated by the light of modern research, its historical associations, the nature of its government, its social advantages and disparagements, nay the very buildings which stood upon the land, and the dialect of its inhabitants, can be accurately learned. In some particulars, indeed, the scene of this part of His earthly course may be obscure, but in regard to the chief of them, and those which reveal most significantly what we wish to ascertain, they are so translucently disclosed that we may clearly see, and distinctly hear, and intelligently hold converse with, the things and persons amidst which, as a Galilean Jew, He lived and moved. What the manner of His life in such a home as that in which He abode, must of necessity have been, has been certified from innumerable sources of information. They send out lights which converge on Nazareth as it was in the days when He was dwelling there, and they mutually attest and interpret one another. So that, carefully combining them, and placing ourselves upon the spot where their blended illumination is poured forth, His living figure, robed in the costume which He actually wore, and surrounded by the circumstances amidst which He habitually moved—comes plainly into view. The vision, which has been so wisely hidden from careless discursive observation, is more and more clearly and vividly defined: it grows in its living reality while we gaze on it, till in many respects we see Him there even more

Reasons of Faith, ch. i.

distinctly than we can see Him afterwards, on the well-known occasions of His active and public ministry, in the towns of Galilee and in Jerusalem.

III. In realising by these means His life throughout that period, dwelling with Him in the house, observing His daily occupations, and His intercourse with His 'kinsfolk and acquaintance,' we obtain most effective help, which is immediately available in carrying out the purpose which we are contemplating.—Then again, this help is increased, our inferences are corrected, and they are also enlarged, by attending to the fuller details of His after life, under the conviction that there was no break in the continuity of its development. And surely this is certain. His course, His habits and proceedings, throughout His public ministry, were the consistent extension and natural issue of His life in His earlier years. His path through Nazareth passed continuously into the more public manifestations of His earthly being, and it was therewith harmoniously blended. This fact is necessarily implied in that consistency and unity which must be ascribed to His habits and proceedings. Every one, therefore, who has looked, under the light of this conviction, into that daily existence in Capernaum and Jerusalem which was, so to speak, interposed between the marked occasions of His ministry, will see reflected in His habits and demeanour there, the life which He had already lived, in another sphere and under other circumstances, in the home of His seclusion. The distinctions which marked him then were afterwards unchanged; and all those precepts which He delivered in His later years had been already practically observed and kept by Him in the years which they succeeded. When this continuity is borne in mind, and when, in the light of it, we read with this backward reference the more detailed pages of His history, we find they cast an enlarging, and also a correcting, illumination on the earlier stage of His existence, and on the scenes and associations amidst which it passed. And this is a source of information which in such an enquiry as that which we are here meditating, should be employed with greatest carefulness.

When it is connected with the others which have been indicated, and when the fragments of information which they supply, are 'carefully attended to, compared and pursued;' when even the obscurest hints which they furnish, are thus 'diligently traced'—clear and definite, and also

<small>Butler's *Analogy*, ubi sup.</small>

authentic, conclusions may be obtained concerning the subject of our enquiry. Just views of the Incarnation and of its Purposes, of Christ as being the 'Similitudo exemplaris totius naturæ,' of His Life as the Light of Men, require us diligently to use the above-mentioned sources of information, while we observe that temper and those rules of enquiry the need of which appears to be expressively indicated by the reserve of the Evangelists. Such an use of these informants has nowhere been forbidden; and their existence, in the absence of any prohibition of the kind, is surely an indication that they were meant to be employed. They show that we should gather instruction from this page, also, of the Revealing Word; though hitherto, from what may surely be called our strange neglect of it, it has been blank and inexpressive.

Divine Kingdom, ubi sup.

In this belief, then, we will look in the direction which has been pointed out, and carefully 'pursue and compare' the intimations of which we have spoken. And we shall undoubtedly find that they marvellously illuminate the fuller and more familiar pages of the Evangelists. They will enable us to approach Christ in the after scenes of His ministry, with a deeper and more vivid sense of His actual Personality. His relations with men

Infra, ch. vi.

will be widened in our view, and we shall perceive fresh aspects of His character, and a fuller significance both in the language of His teaching, and in its illustrations. Moreover, His Divine, as well as Human nature will come before us more impressively: we shall not only understand Him better, and get a profounder insight into many of the purposes of His Work and Ministry, but we shall also find our reverence towards His character deepened, while we are growing more familiar with His Person and demeanour. We shall obtain, besides, a truer apprehension of the nature of our appointed course, and of His nearness and sympathy while it is being faithfully pursued. Its commonest duties will be ennobled in our view, and we shall be stilled in our frequent restlessness under what may so often be very naturally looked upon as its deep and sad humiliations.

Heb. ii. 17, 18; iv. 15, 16.

Moreover, besides this general result from the enquiries which we are meditating, we shall find certain lessons supplied by them that appear to have a special adaptation to the age. Events which are now happening have 'opened out and ascertained,' if we may here use Butler's words in another application of them—'the meaning' of this heretofore strangely neglected portion of the

Analogy, ubi sup.

Redeemer's history. And from that quiet and unobserved, that "unhasting, yet ever unresting" life amidst the Galilean hills, come the very admonitions which our time and people need, and which will calm, while they rebuke, the turmoil and excitement by which our age is painfully distinguished. Those admonitions come to us, solemnly and yet gently and benignantly, condemning the selfishness which is so fearfully weakening our family, social, and national relations, as well as the absorption in present interests which is hiding from men the Supernatural Order in which this sphere of their existence is incorporated, while it also separates them from past ages, and unfits and indisposes them to look onwards with far-reaching interest into the future.

Infra, ch. vii.

Appendix, Note E.

We surely need these admonitions. And here, along with other valuable lessons, we shall find them, if we will turn towards that scene with reverent heedfulness, and diligently use the instruments through which the vision it reveals may be made known. Then it will come forth with unexpected clearness and impressiveness; and we shall feel that its many uses have amply justified the efforts through which it has been unfolded.

CHAPTER I.

INFANCY AND EARLY CHILDHOOD IN NAZARETH.

WE begin then by endeavouring to obtain a distinct view of the material framework of the Divine Life, and of the social circumstances which surrounded it, through the period to which our attention is directed. They are easily described. An unbroken and unquestioned tradition represents Christ's early dwelling-place in Galilee as standing in the last of those open mountain valleys which lie in the course of one who is travelling southward over the westernmost of the two hilly ranges that are thrown off in that direction from Mount Hermon. This western range runs parallel with the sea-coast, overhanging the Phœnician territory through the greater part of its extension; and, just before breaking down abruptly into the Esdraelon plain, it sinks into a green hollow, closed in on all sides, upon which, centuries before the

Stanley's *Sinai and Palestine*, ch. ii. and x.

C

period when Nazareth is first mentioned, communities must have been settled.

Its position is so favourable for man's habitation that none of the upland plains that were traversed by the migratory bands of Hamites, as they came on in this direction from their primeval dwelling, offered greater advantages as a place of settlement. Doubtless it was in the hands of some of those Amorite or Highland descendants of theirs, whom the Israelites were commanded to exterminate, when it was assigned to Zebulon in the tribal division of the country. Surrounded by gently rising and well-wooded hills, fertile and abundantly watered, in a genial and bracing climate, and standing about a thousand feet above the level of the closely adjacent sea—the site of Nazareth enjoyed every one of the advantages which had been promised to the tribe in whose inheritance it was included. From its rich pasture land Zebulon could 'offer his sacrifices of righteousness;' while, close by, he 'sucked of the abundance of the seas, and of the treasures hid in the sand.' Over the roads which led northwards into the Buttauf plain, or down in an opposite direction through the narrow winding passes that conduct to Esdraelon, his families went forward to take part in the conflicts under Barak, and Deborah, and Gideon. Nor could they have held themselves aloof from any of the stirring scenes which were witnessed during the later Jewish history. Living close upon Jezreel and Samaria, those earlier inhabitants of the Nazareth valley would necessarily take their full share in the political and warlike movements with which the Old Testament has made us familiar. In peaceful seasons they were near enough for commercial intercourse with the Phœnicians, whose chief settlement at Tyre was only thirty miles distant. Interchanges of their field produce for the arms and wares of those traders, would naturally go forward even in the centuries when the Hebrew national spirit was mightiest. And as it waned, the Gentile influences, which wrought upon all the dwellers on those Galilean hills, and especially on those among them whose homes bordered on the maritime settlements, took their full effect on the people who lived on the ground we are surveying.

Scripture Lands, p. 176.

In all its forms of life, in its modes of thought and intercourse, and in its social habits, that part of Northern Palestine became more and more deeply marked by the features of whatever nation was then paramount in its sway over the Jewish ground and people. Hence it was that the time when Nazareth emerges from the obscurity of its past history, and comes prominently into notice, a Greco-Roman aspect largely characterized the inhabitants of the town, their buildings, the social customs and the domestic habits of their life, nay, even the language in which their intercourse was carried forward.

Scripture Lands, p. 256.

Among the communities further south that influence had been resisted. Thus a distinctly Jewish aspect predominated almost everywhere throughout Judea; and even in the towns and villages of Samaria, the Grecising influence was comparatively feeble. But, north of the Esdraelon plain, it was, with all the tastes wherewith it was associated, in complete ascendancy. This might be perceived in the people's common intercourse. The speech of a Galilean 'betrayed him,' not only by its provincial uncouthness, but by its frequent use of Greek words and turns of phraseology, which had been naturally introduced through the general prevalence of that language in his neighbourhood. Its distinction in this and similar respects from Judea, was necessarily consequent on the proximity of the Northern province to the Greek settlements, for, while Judea leant upon the desert, Galilee was close to

Matt. xxvi. 73; Luke xxii 59.

the Hellenic communities that depended upon Antioch. Moreover, the personal tastes of the two new rulers of this district of Palestine encouraged the tendency; as was seen, for example, when Philip changed the name of Banias into Cæsarea-Philippi, and there celebrated the rites of Greek and Roman worship in the temple which Herod had erected. Further south he had replaced the Hebrew Bethsaida by the Latin Julias; while his brother Antipas raised the city of Tiberias over an ancient Hebrew cemetery in the same neighbourhood. Close by, on the other side of the Jordan, the names of Gadara, Hippos, and other cities of the Decapolis, with the buildings, especially the large theatres, contained in them, indicated the same tendency. Sepphoris, standing on the plain just in front of Nazareth, on its north-western side, became Dio-Cæsarea. And, in fact, the whole country into which the traveller entered who came from southern Palestine up through the winding passes that led into the town, was becoming more and more 'Galilee of the Gentiles.'[1]

Scripture Lands, p. 282.

---

[1] Over the whole of North Palestine there were numerous signs of that 'exotic civilization' which had been introduced under the Seleucidæ, and which Herod systematically extended. 'Temples, theatres, gymnasia, some of them built on the largest scale, and in a style of the greatest magnificence, hemmed in the narrow home of

It was natural that the upper classes should be most influenced by what might have been justly described as a contagion ; though, in some instances, Hebrew fidelity was maintained among them, as the mention of certain 'chief Pharisees' in the neighbourhood bears witness. In its resistance of the prevailing influences it had, however, its chief refuge, not among 'the lords, high captains, and chief estates' of the province, but rather among the humbler classes, the craftsmen in the towns, the peasantry of the numerous villages, the fishermen upon the lake. While their neighbours flocked to swell the crowds in Herod's theatres, they kept themselves apart ; going up, from time to time, in small companies, to the festivals of the Holy City. And moved in those pilgrimages by the historical and

Luke ii. 41.
John vii. 8, 10.

Judaism. Nor, indeed, were even those restricted boundaries respected by the half pagan monarch. Even the Holy City itself was not exempted from these intrusions of heathenism, but was compelled to smother her resentment while a theatre and, still worse, an amphitheatre, profaned her precincts.' Many tokens of these foreign influences are still extant, not far from Nazareth, in the eastern portion of the district in which it was included. The numerous changes in the occupation of the country, and the war devastations which have swept over it, have obliterated almost every trace of the buildings which existed in Christ's time in His immediate neighbourhood. But even now the ruins of two large theatres, adapted to 'the reception and entertainment of many thousand spectators,' may be seen just south of Tiberias, and about twenty miles from Nazareth.—Dr. Traill's *Josephus*, vol. 1. p. xxxvi.

sacred associations of the scenes through which they had to pass, they would naturally confer together in strenuous protest, nay, often in rebellious discontent, upon the tokens which indicated, so ominously in their view, the fatalest apostasy. Nor can we doubt that, amongst the worthiest examples of these 'faithful amongst the faithless found,' we may reckon Joseph and Mary, along with the families of which they were members.

In the midst of that widely spread apostasy, they kept their 'consciences undefiled,' bravely upholding the trust and testimony which they knew had been Divinely committed to their charge. And we may fairly reckon ancestral influences amongst those through the power of which they also, like their relatives, Zacharias and Elizabeth, 'were righteous before God, walking in all the commandments and ordinances of the Lord blameless.' Luke i 6.

They were both of the 'house and lineage of David;' and this distinction gave a certain honourable high-minded firmness to their consistent support of their profession. Moreover, they were remarkable for their virtues and devoutness. In the few glimpses which have been given of Joseph Luke ii. 4. Cf. Lange's *Life of Christ*, vol. i. p. 381.

we can clearly discern an upright, self-governed, large-hearted, generous man. Mary, his 'espoused wife,' we know more intimately, though, with what must be regarded as a seemly and most instructive reticence, she is on no occasion obtruded in the history, but, on the contrary, is very seldom even mentioned. Still, when she has been disengaged and set clear from the illusions which fictitious legends and weak poetic sentiment have cast around the few occasions on which she is brought forward—we can recognise her distinctly enough for every useful purpose. An affectionately considerate woman; pondering things with heartfelt and not merely intellectual interest; her mind filled with devout thoughts and recollections, as her ready use of Scripture phraseology bears witness; meek, trustful, lovingly submissive to the Divine ordering of her affairs, yet strong, energetic and courageous in doing her part in their accomplishment—Mary stands forward the very ideal of one of the daughters and mothers of Israel. She was a worthy countrywoman of Miriam and Deborah and Hannah, formed and moulded after the highest type of Hebrew character, and yet distinguished by all sweetly feminine qualities in her tenderness and trust.

One can imagine the home, frugal and well-ordered, and yet never coarse or squalid, which such a husband and wife would gather around them, and we know the spirit in which it was administered. In its tone, and in all its circumstances, that sense of their royal ancestry which marked its godly and high-minded occupants, with the obligations that were thence entailed on them—would make itself perceptible. And now, thinking of this Home, and of the place and circumstances in which it was established, remembering the cheerful though not marked or exciting features of Nazareth, and of the country around it, where nature is ever in animated, though nowhere in awful guise; recalling its local surroundings and historical associations; thus thinking of Mary and Joseph's dwelling in their own city, we see where God was manifested in human flesh, where the Life which is the Light of men was developed and made known.

CHAP. I.

Appendix, Note C.

John i. 14.

It was not only for the purpose of presenting human nature afresh in its aboriginal typal form, as it had perfectly reflected the Divine Image, but for the purpose also of showing how man's course in this world should be pursued, that the Second Person of the Blessed Trinity, even the Everlasting Word, was there 'manifested in the flesh.' Nor can we imagine any place, any more than we can think of any time, that was better fitted for carrying out the purposes of His appearing. In the exhaustion of all forms of human error, and the earnest aspirations of men for teaching from above, the 'fulness of the time' for the promised Incarnation, is immediately recognised. And when we think of Nazareth in comparison with all other possible localities in which the earthly life of Christ might have been manifested, the fitness of place is equally apparent. In lonelier scenes, in a wilderness seclusion such as that wherein the Baptist 'waxed strong in spirit' amidst the discipline prepared for him, the materials and instruments for accomplishing the Messiah's purpose were evidently wanting. He could not there have discharged the relationships and fulfilled the duties which were involved in His commission. And, in more public localities, on the great highways of the world, in Cæsarea or Tiberias, nay, even in Jerusalem, there were exceptional circumstances, artificial modes of life, that would have interfered with, and have spoiled the completeness of the pattern. Nazareth, standing, as we may say, near the centre of the age's movements, nay, even within view of them, and yet so placed as to be exempted from their undue influence and pressure, furnished a scene than which we can imagine none better fitted for the reception and entertainment of the Divine Redeemer, and for the supply of the instruments which He needed for discharging this part of His benignant mission among men.

Upon the ineffably mysterious occurrence through which He took our humanity upon Himself, we stay not to remark, except with the observation that it was in seemly, and indeed needful, congruity with His Character, and with the Purposes that we have ascribed to Him. We must feel that we are, indeed, among the harmonies of God, when, bearing that Character and those Purposes in our remembrance, we listen heedfully to the announcement —'The Holy Ghost shall come upon thee, and the Power of the Highest shall overshadow thee.' Just such an entrance into man's framework and circumstances, befitted the Redeemer's Nature, and the ends of His deep humiliation.

And this sense of congruity, this satisfaction of every mind which dwells thoughtfully on the circumstances of the event, is greatly deepened when we observe the fitness for their part of those who were chosen as the agents in its accomplishment. Apart from their native qualifications, they were also

Liddon's Bamp. Lect. Lect. v.

Luke i. 35.

marvellously wrought upon, so that their adaptation to the work assigned to them might be perfected. The circumstances connected with the Incarnation brought the severest trials both on Joseph and on Mary. His trustful generosity was exercised and proved by those trials, and so also were her courage and her submissiveness. 'Behold the handmaid of the Lord. Be it unto me,' whatever the suspicion and contumely of which I am the object—still 'Be it unto me according to thy word.' The suffering brought on by the occasion, bound them yet more closely to one another. Grateful affection on her part, and generous trust on his— trust which was so justified and strengthened by the portents that accompanied the Birth—secured and rivetted that mutual love and reverence which are the basis of the home life, and which, as we shall see, were so especially becoming in a purely Jewish household. And these qualities were at once urgently needed to support them in the efforts which they were called upon to make when they removed, for a while, from Bethlehem into Egypt. For there they were in a country wherein— although it was not entirely foreign, since extensive colonies of Jews had been long settled in the land—unusual exertions were required from them, during the two or three years of His earliest infancy. Well deserving our most careful attention is the fact, that it was amidst these efforts, amidst the toils and privations which were necessarily entailed on them by their stay in Egypt, that Mary and Joseph grew into that needful familiarity with the Child, which, with their vivid remembrance of the solemn portents that had attended the Nativity, must have been impossible in the daily monotonous quiet of their home at Nazareth. This arrangement of their affairs continued—through an ordering, the wisdom of which we can well discern—until signs of opening consciousness were witnessed in the Infant. And then, at the end of two or three years, during which their movements are fittingly concealed, He came at length with His parents, as we shall call them, into the home and neighbourhood we have been surveying. There, under the tender and affectionate watchfulness of Mary, who was ever anxiously pondering the wonderful circumstances connected with His Nativity, and instructed and cared for by Joseph—Christ grew up, through His infant years, amidst the circumstances of a home which was in the likeness of one of those whereof we read so often in the after history. We may gather a distinct conception of the carpenter's house from the domestic allusions which we meet with in the fuller pages of the narrative, and may thence learn its form, its aspect and accommodations. In such a house He lived, 'waxing strong in spirit,' culturing and manifesting to 'His kinsfolk and acquaintance' in Nazareth, the understanding which, even in His early boyhood, excited so much wonder in Jerusalem. Nature in all her aspects and vicissitudes, the changing sky and seasons, the plains, the distant mountains—and Hermon, with its snowy summit, was in view—the neighbouring sea, the employments of the men around Him and their converse, were all educating, were gradually drawing out, the mind, the affections, which appertained to the Humanity which had been assumed by Him.

Brief as are the notices of those early years, they are enough for an assurance which is beyond questioning, that they carried Him forward in true and actual contact with the common circumstances and transactions of human life in that time and place. And therefore we need not imagine, for we know, how His individuality was realised to Himself while those years went forward. Through familiar intercourse with His thoughtful, high-minded, devout mother, as they sat together in the house and as they walked through the lonely passes that led downwards from their mountain valley, or stood on that hill-top which brought into their view those historical sites on the associations of which she would naturally, with all the enthusiasm of one of David's daughters, dwell; by this intercourse, and by the graver and more measured teachings of Joseph, as he 'sat with Him in the house, and talked with Him by the way'— the human intellect of our Blessed Lord came through ordinary channels into definite and realised possession of that knowledge which had dwelt substantially, potentially, within His soul from the beginning.[2] So, again, the movements which were going on around Him; the labours of the craftsmen in their workshops; the agriculture of the neighbouring fields; the commerce of which, whenever He ascended the hill-top beside His dwelling, the signs were witnessed in the ships that whitened the neighbouring ocean, and the slowly-pacing caravans that moved across the adjacent plain; the political disturbances and outbreaks that were constantly troubling Galilee, and which naturally centred round Herod's capital

Infra, chap. iv.

Deut. xi. 19.

Cf. note p. 84.

---

[2] On Christ's 'increase in knowledge,' see Appendix.

of Sepphoris, whose buildings glistened on the northern plain which there came within His view—all, in the same way, augmented His knowledge, and enlarged His consciousness. Coming thus into possession of the copious imagery which was afterwards reproduced in His teaching,[3] He also gradually obtained a deeper sense of His personal individual life towards God, and of the relations into which it brought Him with other partakers of existence. His understanding opened, His soul 'waxed strong' through His docile reception of the influences and instructions conveyed to it while He exercised that true childlike spirit which He afterwards commended, and which He then exemplified by submitting Himself in loving trust to all who had claims upon His confidence.

Luke ii. 40.

---

[3] 'It was there, in the fields below the village, that He had watched how the lilies grew, and seen with what a gorgeous dress, in colouring above kingly purple, their Creator had clothed them. There, in the gardens, He had noticed how the smallest of all the seeds grew into the tallest of herbs. There, outside the house, He had seen two women grinding at one mill; inside, a woman hiding the leaven in the dough. There, in the market-place, He had seen the five sparrows sold for two farthings. The sheep walks of the hills, and vineyards of the valleys had taught Him what were the offices of the good shepherd, and the careful vinedresser; and all the observations of those thirty years were treasured up, to be drawn upon in due time, and turned into the lessons by which the world was to be taught wisdom.'—DR. HANNA'S *Earlier Years of Our Lord*, p. 383.

In those exercises of meekness and docility, through which He thus entered into the position that had been prepared for Him, we see the first phase of that manifestation of the typal Life which is the Light of men, and which it was His mission to disclose. In our view of Him as a 'little child,' manifesting in that character the faith through which intelligence comes, and obtaining the intelligence which is the reward of it,[4] we see, in clearest development, how the younger inheritors of being everywhere are meant to take possession of their individuality, and to fit themselves for inheriting the accumulated experience and insight of their elders; and how also they become qualified for accomplishing the duties, and struggling in the conflicts, and for occupying, in all other respects, the place and the relationships that are prepared for them.

It was by means of these relationships, as well as through the more general influences which wrought upon His human spirit, that He came into definite possession of man's personal life, and disclosed its true embodiment. Through the connexions into which, accordingly, He entered, we

Mark x. 15; 1 Pet. ii. 2.

---

[4] 'Crede ut intelligas. Intellectus enim merces est fidei.'—St. Augustine.

shall now follow Him, and observe His discharge of their duties and obligations, while 'He increased in wisdom, and waxed strong in spirit,' by means of them, thus manifesting the consummate Pattern of that Life which has been appointed for mankind.

CHAPTER II.

HOME AND FAMILY LIFE IN NAZARETH.

THE fulfilment of His purpose in exemplifying the typal form of created being, and by this means setting forth a Life which should be the 'Light of men,' made it necessary that He should enter into every one of man's relationships. One of the main ends of His Incarnation was to show how 'portions of our individual existence become subjected to the laws and conditions of more general life,' and for what ends that which 'is thus sacrificed has been thrown into a common fund.' And the first of the organic connections into which He entered with this view, is the Home Life—the Life through which every man is appointed to pass as the member of a family and household.

This Home Life appears to form an essential part, not of man's condition only, but of the Divine Order of the Universe; and there is reason to believe

Divine Kingdom, p. 26.

that it is out of families, as their elementary constituents, that larger societies and associations have universally been formed. Is not this fact betokened by the Fatherly name of God? And does it not follow from the statement that the heirs of immortal being have been created in the 'Image of the Son'? The domestic constitution appears indeed, to be grounded in the Divine Nature. Nor is its existence indistinctly betokened by the mention of societies existing elsewhere in the universe, such as can hardly be looked upon as a mere aggregate of individuals. The 'thrones and dominions,' the 'principalities and powers,' of which we are told, surely imply an earlier association of their members in households; and indeed the existence of such households appears to be explicitly affirmed when we read of the 'fatherhoods of heaven' in connection with those of earth. Moreover, with these intimations on the subject, the notices of man in his still unfallen state, when he was brought into association with the sinless communities of the Divine Kingdom, are very strikingly accordant. And so also is the signal honour attributed to the household tie throughout the inspired history of men, for does it not continually remind us that 'God setteth the solitary in families?'

Nor should we omit to add to these reasons for believing in the universal prevalence throughout the Divine Kingdom of the domestic constitution, its fitness—nay, we may even say, its indispensable needfulness—for the moral and intellectual training of the younger inheritors of being. Their exercises of self-control and of humility in this position, prepare them for meeting the larger requirements of law; while the efforts of trustful love which it demands, give them individual possession of the treasures of knowledge and sentiment which belong to their community. We may observe too that, besides fitting its members for wider relationships, it aids in their personal development: by means of their family ties they obtain a fuller and firmer possession of their own consciousness. Life truly lived in the household brings out the individual life in richer development, besides qualifying each member for a larger range of activity and an intenser fulness of emotion.

When these considerations are borne in mind, we can hardly question that life in the family may be looked upon as an essential portion of the heavenly pattern of existence; and, consequently, that its living manifestation in normal and complete development entered into the mission which the

[margin: CHAP. II.]
[margin: Lament. iii. 27.]
[margin: Divine Kingdom, p. 27.]

Eternal Word became Incarnate to fulfil. Nor can we imagine any circumstances in which it could have been exemplified more perfectly than in those of a Jewish family, and especially of a family such as we know that of Joseph and Mary must have been, when we bear in mind the remarkable position which they occupied.

In a Jewish household we find all the influences and arrangements that are required for the elementary development of moral natures. The ideal family and home life of man had been obscured, 'its heavenly pattern' had been spoiled by his apostasy; and one of the ends of those special communications which God has conveyed to him from the beginning, has been its restoration according to its original design. When accordingly we look into the Mosaic ordinances, and learn what were the general habits and tone of domestic life amongst the Jews, we find, as might have been expected, the very ideal of Home realised. In that guarded sacredness of its relationships which is so significantly marked by the genealogies of the Old Testament, and the manifestation of which was doubtless one of the reasons for inserting them; in the authority belonging to both parents; in the tenderness and care enjoined on them, and the reciprocal obedience and trust required from their children—we see provisions for that very condition of household duty and relationship which might be looked for in the homes of the unfallen. What the πατριαὶ of heaven are, the Jewish πατριὰ was meant to be.¹ And such, in fact, it almost was in those old Hebrew families which Joseph and Mary, as 'Israelites indeed,' would regard as their standard and example. For it would be in the very spirit as well as habits of the fathers of their people, that they would obey the domestic ordinances which the Law enjoined, and which the prophets had enforced by the strongest exhortations, as well as by emphatic warnings of the results which would surely follow, in this instance, from neglect and disobedience.

Ephes. iii. 15.

Isaiah xlv. 10.

---

¹ The carefully guarded sacredness of their family life may be clearly discerned throughout the history of the Jewish people. Seen first in the households of the patriarchs, and then during the abode of the people in Egypt, we find it afterwards systematically ordered and secured by the laws of Moses. The chief *distinctions* of his domestic legislation, after carefully providing for the purity of the household (Levit. xviii.; Deut. xxvii.), were these: (1) Authority over their children was shared by *both* parents (Levit. xx. 9; Deut. xxi. 19); (2) While reverent obedience was strictly required from children towards their parents, affectionate heedfulness on the parents' parts towards them, was equally demanded (Deut. vi. 7, xi. 19; Psalm lxxviii. 5–7); (3) Only through the family, as son and brother, and as husband, could the Hebrew take any part in the business of the nation (Numb. i. 4, xxvi. 2).

Moreover, in Joseph's position at Nazareth, where he was placed in the very front of those heathenising influences, against which such a man would be severely and unrelentingly intolerant, all the characteristic distinctions of a Jewish household would be brought out, and its peculiar features rigorously insisted on. Conscientious, earnest son of David as he was, he would feel himself called on to maintain an inexorable protest against the laxity prevailing in his neighbourhood. His home, therefore, would be eminently fitted for the manifestation of that typal example of family life which was to be exhibited therein. And this will be recognised more clearly, when we examine its particulars, and follow Christ in the discharge of His household duties; first, in the early part of His course, where they were chiefly marked by subordination and submissiveness; and then in the later, and, as we shall see, the more active and arduous, sphere of their fulfilment.

Looking, then, at the earlier developments of His household life, we are first reminded that 'He was subject to His parents.' He 'honoured His father and mother,' implicitly trusting them, as the words imply, and submitting Himself lovingly to their behests. Recognising the paternal authority as representative of the authority of God, and its utterances as the utterances which came nearest to Him of the Law by which the Divine Order is maintained, He sacredly obeyed it; and, in a godly spirit, He subjected His human will and wishes, and conformed all the details of His household life, to its requirements. In a home restricted by special limitations as His was, with narrow resources, and commonplace, if not rude, and ungenial companionship, daily and hourly occasions would arise for efforts of self-control, for submissive yieldings to the will of those around Him, for acts of kindly concession to their infirmities. And all these occasions were faithfully and cheerfully met; the duties involved in them were discharged lovingly and punctually. We may be sure that gentleness, and tender consideration for the needs of others, ever marked His demeanour in the household. Nor were the ordinary influences of individual self-will alone resisted, but those also which might have taken the guise of religious scruples and pious conscientiousness. Under no pretexts of devotion did He withhold from His parents anything by which they might have been lawfully 'profited' by His means. In this matter He showed no morbid rigidity: He was not 'righteous overmuch;' but

Divine Kingdom, p. 190.

Matt. xv. 5.

in spirit and truth, He then set forth, in His own practice, that teaching respecting the Corban plea which He afterwards declared in words.

Nor was it only in trustful dependence on His parents, and submission to their authority, that the laws of family life were typally observed in His demeanour. Such observance was also shown by His familiar and fraternal intercourse with those who were in the same position as His own. We say 'fraternal' intercourse, because, whatever was the relationship which actually subsisted between Him and those who are spoken of as 'His brethen and sisters,' every allusion to that intercourse shows its closeness and its intimacy.[2] Evidently he lived an undistinguished life in the midst of them. Sharing cheerfully in their interests and engagements, He was also patient with their infirmities, and heedful of their needs. The statement that Joseph and Mary 'sought Him among their kinsfolk and ac-

[2] Full information on both sides of the much-disputed question as to the nearness of Christ's connection with the other members of His family, is given by Prof. Lightfoot in his *Epist. to Gal.* pp. 247-282. It is worth observing that, while the intimacy of His connection with them, whether brothers and sisters, or cousins, was shown by their being among the last who learned His true character, the fact that they did, at length, yield, and that they acknowledged Him, whom they had regarded as an ordinary relative, to be none other than the Messiah, largely increases the value of their testimony.—*Divine Kingdom*, note p. 188.

quaintance,' perfectly agrees with this conclusion. 'The parents of Christ,' says Bishop Hall, 'knew Him well to be of a disposition, not strange nor sullen or stoical, but sweet and sociable; and therefore they do not suspect that He had wandered into the solitary fields; they supposed He had spent the time and the way in the company of their friends and neighbours.' Moreover, it is further illustrative of the same fact, that they, even His own 'kinsfolk and acquaintance,' were among the people who had most difficulty in recognising His Messiahship. It is said that 'neither did His brethren and sisters believe on Him.' Was not that unbelief of theirs markedly significant of such an actual simple participation by Him in their common life, as that which we have indicated? They could not think of One who had taken part in their daily occupations, and who, it may be, had even shared in their amusements, as being so unspeakably higher than themselves.

Yes: in fulfilment of His mission, He sincerely and habitually took part in their engagements, and was concerned in all their interests. Embodying all this department of human life in a heavenly spirit, 'in the Lord,' and according to God's will, as His Apostle afterwards enjoined—He was

Contemplations, On N. T. Book II.

Ephes. vi. 1.

in this respect, emphatically, 'like unto His brethren.'

Nor is this true only with reference to the privacy of home life, and the duties which He was called on to discharge therein. It was seen in public developments, on occasions of mourning and festivity. That funeral which He met, not far from Nazareth, at the gate of Nain, could not have been the only scene of that description at which He had been present. Nor could it either have been an unusual circumstance in His history, when He was afterwards invited with His companions to a marriage feast. The habits of His public life, the illustrations and allusions of His teaching, betoken familiarity with everything that took place on occasions of this kind—with all their incidents, and with the feelings, good and evil, that were brought out by them. We are here referring to His presence at festal gatherings, like that in Levi's house; and to His parables, such as that of the wedding guests; as well as to His admonitions against the obtrusive selfishness, the vulgar pushings for precedence, which, no doubt, He had often witnessed in such scenes.

We plainly gather these suggestions as to His demeanour in His earlier and youthful course, and amidst those occasions on which acts of submissiveness and subordination were required from Him. But, further on in His path, in His early manhood, when circumstances demanded His strenuous discharge of the more active and arduous duties which grow out of the domestic relationships, there are plain indications that these requirements also were faithfully and punctually fulfilled. Every injunction concerning the more active services of filial piety which is laid down in the Old Testament, was faithfully obeyed, and its highest examples — in His laborious care for His parents, and for those of His kindred who naturally looked to Him for help and counsel — appeared in His demeanour. In His discharge of all the family obligations that were appropriate to the later years of the period about which we are now thinking, the 'commandment of God was not made void by Him;' and He duly rendered everything whereby His family might be 'profited' by His exertions. Definite illustrations of this statement are suggested, if they are not explicitly furnished, by the narrative. It has always been held that the silence of the Evangelists respecting Joseph after his appearance at the visit to Jerusalem, can only be explained by his death at some period before Christ's public

Levit. xix. 3.
Deut. xxvii. 16.
1 Samuel xxii. 3.

ministry began.³ And from this it follows that the support of His mother, and the care and government of their household, had, and possibly for many years, exclusively devolved on Him. It is plainly in accordance with this conclusion that He is spoken of as 'the carpenter,' implying that He was in a position wherein He had to meet the duties of the 'good man of the house,' in the position which Joseph had previously occupied.

These conclusions may be securely drawn respecting His family course during the thirty years of which we are speaking. And these characteristic features of His life are brought out more fully when we bear in mind the disturbing influences which operated there, in that time and place, and which had such a tendency to loosen family ties and obligations. We here refer to the excitements and enterprises of the age, as well as to the corruptions prevailing over Gentile Galilee, which appeared to call for instant protest and resistance,

---

³ That Joseph died before Christ's public ministry began, is plainly implied by the absence of any mention of him in the Evangelists' narrative of that period, as well as by the emphatic designation of Christ as a carpenter (Mark vi. 3). And indeed the fact seems be explicitly intimated by His commendation of Mary to the care of St. John, who was commanded to receive her as his mother, in consequence of which command, and 'from that hour, he took her to his own home' (John xix. 26, 27).

and which found the focus of their attractiveness and power, only a few miles from His dwelling, in the neighbouring court of Antipas at Sepphoris, full within His view. We feel at once indeed that the merely dissipating influences that surrounded His position could have had no power over Him. 'One look from His majestic brow, Seated as on the top of Virtue's hill, Discountenanced' them all. But then, what wrongs were being perpetrated within His observation! What errors were then proclaimed that seemed to call aloud for His instant protest and denial! Indeed, every motive that has at any time unduly, though nobly, led men away from home ties and obligations, presented themselves to His human spirit in that place and hour.

Nevertheless, to these He firmly clung through the entire period, because they had the first claims on Him; and it was by their discharge, carried forward in such a spirit as we have witnessed, that His individual existence was raised and perfected. Under Joseph's godly administration of his household, every member of it was regarded, in the old Jewish spirit, as having been also incorporated with a Fellowship of which God Himself is Head. And this view and feeling was reciprocated

CHAP. II.

Appendix, Note B.

Paradise Regained, book ii.

on the part of the 'Holy Child Jesus,' and shown by Him in acts of deference and courtesy, as well as of reverent submissiveness, all through His earlier years, as well as afterwards in that later period, when the care and oversight of the house probably devolved on Him. It was in this 'obedience to His parents in the Lord,' and this mindfulness of the wants and infirmities of those who were 'heirs together with Him of the grace of life,' that He 'waxed strong in spirit,' and 'increased in favour with God.' Thus He grew into the character which was afterwards recognised by the 'Voice from Heaven,' 'This is my beloved Son in Whom I am well pleased.'

Thus looking to the home in Nazareth, as it is presented to us by our knowledge of the place and its surroundings, and holding firmly the assurance that He therein embodied and reflected the habits of the celestial πατριαί, and observed the precepts which had been inculcated by Moses and the Prophets, and which were afterwards set forth afresh by His Apostles—we may be certain that He thus honoured His father and mother, receiving their instruction, and even submitting meekly to their rebukes when He was misunderstood by them. We know, too, that He was thus 'kindly affectioned' towards His brethren, bearing their burdens, covering their infirmities, mourning with them in their sorrows, and rejoicing in their joys. Moreover, these unquestionable certainties respecting His earlier years, are still further illustrated when we examine His after life and teaching, with the purpose of thence obtaining that retrospective light which may reveal more clearly, and make us more familiar with, the period under our review.

We know then that in Capernaum, as well as in Jerusalem and Bethany, considerable portions of His time were passed amidst the intercourse, the employments and relaxations, of the families whose members there gathered round Him. Nor can it be questioned that His domestic life in this later period, was uniform with, was the consistent extension of, previous habits of the same kind during the years we are considering. In those friendly households, He observed his old usages, though no longer owning a home which bore His name, as His touching words, 'the Son of man hath not where to lay His head,' remind us so pathetically. The familiarity and frequency of His references at that time to the common incidents of family existence, to the domestic economy in every part

Matt. viii. 14.
Luke x. 38.

Matt. xxiii. 25.
Mark iv. 21.

of it, to the daily customs, nay even to the ordinary utensils, of the house—show in what associations and habits He had been previously living. That tenderness, also, and consideration which was manifested in His home intercourse during the later period, must have distinguished Him throughout the earlier. His 'kinsfolk and acquaintance' would remark that just what He was then, He had always been. And, along with the kindness and modesty, the noble self-repression and control, which was ever mindful of the wants and feelings of those that were nearest to Him in His home, we may well connect His unbroken calmness, His habitual freedom from disturbance. Those injunctions which he delivered afterwards concerning the μερίμναι βιωτικαῖ, the life distractions of family existence, had long been practised amidst the narrow means, the humiliating cares and perplexities, of a poor man's household. Here, especially, in His later habits and injunctions, we see what His earlier course must have been amidst all domestic 'troubles and adversities,' when He 'cast His care' on His Father who was 'caring for Him.' Often, doubtless, at the table, and by the fireside, of the Nazareth household that familiar scene in the house at Bethany had been anticipated.

Yes: there too, amidst the humiliating anxieties and perplexities of His household, the solemn reproof had frequently been heard, '*Thou art careful and troubled about many things.' Nor do I blame thee for an earnest regard to them, since they belong to our family life, and to these domestic bonds. Only keep their place in relation to the 'one thing needful' constantly in view. Administer them from the soul's true centre. Think of them as they are explained by the great object of human life, by the reason why you have been called into existence and placed on earth, and been summoned to these duties. In the light of that high purpose look on all your obligations, and regard and administer them with that purpose constantly in view.*

With such unbroken calmness, He lived out the appointed course through which every inheritor of being in the Divine Kingdom is prepared for wider spheres of life and service. Thus were the order and purity, the love and serenity and blessedness of the heavenly 'fatherhoods' completely reflected in His person and proceedings. Nor was the reflection ever disturbed by the influences then surrounding Him, which so mightily tended to mar the embodiment, and destroy its influence and its instructiveness. We need hardly

John xiv. 27.

Luke xii. 44.

remark with what a high sanction and solemn authority He thus surrounded the earliest and most elementary constituent of the organic unions into which men have been incorporated. That in the 'Life which was the Light of men,' because in it the Divine Economy was perfectly reflected —the family existence was thus lived out in all its parts and aspects, and in the most difficult scenes of its development, confirms, with a proof from which there is no appeal, our assurance that the discharge of home duties and relationships is the first and most incumbent of the obligations which devolve upon mankind.

And it may well be added, that His 'waxing strong in spirit' amongst those duties, and there 'increasing in favour with God and man,' is a certain token that in household life man's individual existence may be perfected. There the noblest qualifications and the firmest strength may be obtained: there men may be fitted for the highest and most arduous duties that can ever devolve upon them in the larger spheres into which families have been incorporated.

Supra, p. 56.

CHAPTER III.

LIFE IN THE NAZARETH COMMUNITY.

THE next outlying sphere wherein faculties and affections that have been trained in this manner, are exercised, is found in the united aggregate of the families which are dwelling in any well-defined locality. In this aggregate, which we distinguish as the community, all the households of that neighbourhood are connected; and unions of this kind enter into the still vaster and more general forms of the Divine Order. Of this Order they are the essential constituents; and into one of them, therefore, Christ entered during the period we are surveying.

In virtue of that same law of mutual compensation and helpfulness out of which families originate, communities, villages and cities have been constituted. From the nature of their constitution, households must thus join and blend with one another. And looking further outward, it may also be affirmed that the existence of these larger unions is necessarily implied in those which are still vaster, even in the 'principalities and powers,' the nations and kingdoms, which we know are universally existing. In other words, there is reason for believing that the local associations which lie next outside the families of earth, and include them, are found in all worlds throughout the universe. Certainly they were contemplated as an essential part of the Hebrew polity. And, since this was Divinely framed and constituted, and was administered by a typal people upon a pattern land, it may well be looked upon as the exemplary form after which all States were intended to be fashioned.[1] At all events, it formed a part of the constitution under which Christ lived. Com-

---

[1] The typal, pattern character of Palestine, and also of the Jewish people, is well worth remarking in connexion with our entire subject. 'Set in the midst of all other nations,' the appointed home of the Israelites presented what may well be called an epitome and sampler of them all. And so of the Jew it may be said that in him the temperament of every nation, all the phases of humanity, have been reflected, and that every form of man's development has been seen in his demeanour. Obviously it was in just such circumstances, in such a land and among such a people, that the ideal of humanity could be best embodied, and the entire course of man's life pictured forth in its completeness.—Cf. *Reasons of Faith*, chap. viii.

munities made up of households that were locally adjacent, and then passing, through a natural development, into provinces and nations, are constantly referred to in the statutes of the Hebrew legislator. How far the Mosaic ordinances, under this head, had been modified in Christ's age, among the villages and towns of Palestine; in what manner the communities of Galilee were related to the Nation, so far as the Jewish people formed a nation at that time—is indeed uncertain. There is reason to believe that the municipal affairs of such places were administered by deputies from the Chief Council in Jerusalem, who acted under the control of the Roman Government and of the Herodian princes. Some such management of the civil and ecclesiastical business of Nazareth through the years of which we are now thinking, probably existed. But, whatever its exact nature, we cannot question that civic and corporate, as well as household, life formed part of the Divinely appointed Order under which Christ lived; that He fully entered into it, and took His share of all its burdens and responsibilities.

In this next larger sphere, as well as in the household, He thus fulfilled, or rather embodied, during the years we are thinking of, the maxims

Josephus, Life. Sect. xii.

CHAP. III.

Infra, p. 60

which He Himself afterwards uttered, and which He instructed His Apostles to deliver. All those acts of faithful duty and of active benevolence, those habits of self-restraining and self-devoted tenderness, which we observe in Him during the years of His public ministry, had been already witnessed in that quiet and secluded scene; and the lessons which then were openly taught by Him, and which needed such a sphere as this for their fulfilment, had, through many years before they were thus delivered, been diligently practised by Himself.

Our conviction that His after-life was continuous and uniform with that which He had previously lived, and therefore that His course in those earlier years can be inferred from it, makes this conclusion certain, however freshly the facts which it brings forward may present themselves, through our strange disregard of them, and our neglect of the sources from which we may obtain authentic information on the subject. We are, however, carefully guarded against the impression that His habits, as He so lived in this enlarged sphere of life, were aimless and fruitless, unsystematic and discursive. It is well known that the rules of Jewish life required every member of the community to follow some clearly defined pursuit and occupation. It was then, as it was afterwards, a current maxim among His people, 'He who teacheth not his son a trade, teacheth him to steal.' Moreover, it is expressly said that the 'form of a servant' was characteristically assumed by Him; and we are, besides, distinctly told that He followed the occupation of His reputed father.

CHAP. III.

Luke xxii. 27.
Philipp. ii. 7.

Mark vi. 3.

We know, therefore, that in Joseph's workshop, and in the houses of the town and neighbourhood, where the carpenter's occupation was carried forward—He was employed in steadfast and continuous, in quiet but strenuous toil. There He was engaged on works which afforded better opportunities for associated labour, and which would supply occasions for wider intercourse with His fellow townsmen, than any others to which he could have been appointed.[2] In the very likeness of the true sons of industry, He was thus constantly occupied in

---

[2] In connexion with the obvious fitness of a carpenter's occupation for securing intercourse with His fellow-townsmen, we may observe that it also necessarily involved Him in negotiations outside the limits of His community. Assistance in His work from artisans engaged in connected trades, who were living in the neighbourhood, necessitated intercourse of this description. Moreover purchases of the materials of His craft would take Him to the neighbouring ports, as, e.g., to Ptolemais, which was almost close by, and to Tyre which was about 30 miles distant. In however strange an aspect facts of this kind may present themselves, thoughtful consideration will show that they must be recognised in order duly to appreciate the course of life which Christ at this time pursued.

pursuits which demanded skill and forethought, together with persevering, vigorous endeavour, and which also were productive, and practically helpful to the community of which He was a member. In fact, the very ideal of genuine work was then witnessed in the labours of Him who, in after years, was recognised as 'the carpenter,' and who was ever 'diligent in business,' doing 'with all His might' whatever His hand found then to be done.

It was in this position, as one of the artisans of the town, that He took His place among the inhabitants of Nazareth, sharing their burdens, interesting Himself in their affairs and responsibilities, and using all opportunities of well-doing which occurred to Him. We may here usefully refer again to the commonly accepted inference from the narrative that Joseph died some years before His public ministry began. Now this being so, it follows that His occupations must have been independently pursued through a considerable period for His own support, and for that of His widowed mother. Such a conclusion appears to arise necessarily from certain well-known statements which are made by the Evangelists; and, being accepted, it brings out in marked emphatic illustration that aspect of His life which we are now contemplating. This next outlying sphere of duty must have been perfectly filled out by Him, and in every imaginable part, if, indeed, He occupied for some years, as it so plainly seems He did, a position as the independent master of a household. <small>Mark vi. 3.</small>

It was perfectly fulfilled in every part of it, and all its obligations were discharged, in sedulous and faithful toil, as well as in acts of true beneficence. In other words we know that, all through His abode in Nazareth, He proved Himself to be a 'faithful and wise servant' in the humble position which He therein occupied. Amidst the 'little things' which then engaged Him, His fidelity was manifested. In conscientious toil and service, He then 'rendered to all their dues;' 'custom to whom custom, fear to whom fear, honour to whom honour.' <small>Matt. xxiv. 45. Luke xvi. 10.</small> <small>Rom. xii.</small> Moreover, the duties of beneficence were practised by Him, as well as those of loftiest and most rigorous integrity. He bore the burdens of His neighbours, and promoted, by all means of service and of sympathy, the public welfare of the community into which He had entered. Throughout that time also, and restrained neither by weariness nor by fastidiousness, He 'went about doing good.' When a 'brother trespassed against Him,' He sought to reconcile that brother by all the expedients which <small>Acts x. 38. Matt. xviii. 15.</small>

He afterwards commended. Nor was any unfeeling harshness practised by Him in exacting payment of the debt and service which was owing to Him from those who were fellows in His servitude. No Lazarus lay uncared for at His gate. And if He met any wounded, languishing travellers upon the roads which He then traversed, forthwith those sufferers' wounds were bound up by Himself, and, in tenderest sympathy and foresight, He 'took care of them.' He fed the hungry, and clothed the naked, and visited the sick. Such conclusions respecting his habits may be gathered from our certainty that He had already practised what He taught, and that His habits during His seclusion were consistently uniform with those of His public life and ministry.[3] And with them agree the historical statements which bear upon that period; as, for instance, in that mention of the 'acquaintance' among whom they sought Him, and the increasing 'favour with man' in which He grew up, as well as the general familiarity with His person through

---

[3] This backward reference and use of the precepts which Christ and His apostles delivered concerning the personal and social duties of men in circumstances such as those amidst which He was placed— might be indefinitely extended. In fact thus regarded, such precepts may be read as *historically* descriptive of the Life which He was living throughout those years, and of the temper and method in which every human relationship was discharged by Him.

those earlier years, which is plainly betokened by His after history. All the statements of the Evangelists imply, nay, they plainly indicate, the fact that, as He had not separated Himself in any hermit-like retirement from family life, so, with His domestic, He had perfectly blended a neighbourly, existence in His community, had actively engaged in its business, and had cheerfully accepted its responsibilities.

Thus, still holding fast our conviction that, as Man, He then lived a real human life, from day to day in active intercourse with men, and using all the sources of information which are within our reach—we may securely figure Him, not only passing, as we have seen, through the ordinary routine of home pursuits and intercourse, but also taking His full share in the business and interests of the community—going into the houses of His acquaintance; buying and selling in the market-place; witnessing, nay, even innocently joining in men's festivities; discussing topics of common interest in their assemblies; living a neighbourly and helpful, nay, what we may not unfitly call a humane and genial, as well as beneficent, existence in the midst of them.

Thus He wrought at the works prepared for

Matt. xxvi. 55.

Matt. xi. 19.

CHAP. III.

Ephes. ii. 10.

Him, the works which naturally presented themselves in that place and hour; with those works He was busied, and not with others chosen by Himself. In that quiet town, and among the simple people who were living there, in His workshop, in their houses, He thus laboured, steadfastly and fruitfully, for the good of His community, and for the help and welfare of those with whom He was immediately connected. And so, besides manifesting in this manner the true form of that particular sphere of human life, He also perfectly obeyed, and, in obeying, He typally exemplified, that law of functional service which regards every one as holding in the Divine Order an appointed place which is,

Mark xiii. 34.
1 Pet. iv. 10.

in the most emphatic sense, his own, and in which duties and obligations for promoting the common good have been specially assigned to him.

This law obtains universally, but the stress of its requirements is felt in duties such as those wherewith Christ was occupied in Nazareth, which have been laid upon men in their families and neighbourhoods. And for its perfect realisation and fulfilment, they must have a living perception of the system in which they have been incorporated, and of their own peculiar calling in the midst of it. Beyond their individual life, they must habitually recognise the organic existence which they are sharing, and must perceive the 'historic forces and common laws' by which it is vitally pervaded. Under this recognition, moreover, their efforts must be ruled by submissive patience and strenuous self-control, as well as by an utter trust in that Loving Wisdom governing the movements of the whole framework, which is indeed the immovable ground of its symmetry and fixedness. 'Not my will, O Father, but Thine be done' must be the ruling motto of their lives. In the far-reaching harmonies of the Divine Economy, the results which flow from the efforts of any single agent can be only partially ascertained, and may be altogether hidden and unknown. And this is a trial of affiance, under which all who overlook this view of their 'organic life,' and are possessed by the 'spirit of individualism,' naturally fail. Men of these perceptions and this temper, act instinctively as if the whole results of their activity should be surveyed; and as if they, and not God Himself, were the promoters of His cause. In search of immediate results, and at the impulse of a zeal, which is false and blind, since it rests on a denial of the very fundamental principles of their Divine Association, they go away from homely scenes of

margin: CHAP. III.

Divine Kingdom, chap. iv.

Ephes. i. 11.

toil and self-restraint like that in Nazareth, where their work should be accomplished, to enter into another sphere which may be far apart from that into which they have been called. And thus, instead of realising their place in the great fellowship, and duly accomplishing its works and obligations, its purposes are thwarted and contradicted by their means. Mistrustful of the wisdom which placed them where they are, and which assigned to each one the work that has been given him to do; negligent of all seemly patience and needful self-control, they seek to anticipate the purposes of God, and would even endeavour to improve them. And so, unconscious of the mighty harmonies, and far-reaching symmetry, of the scheme which He is administering, they throw its earthly developments into that confusion wherein they appear so often through the long progress of man's history, and frustrate many of the chief purposes for the accomplishment of which existence has been given.

In other words, they go away from that Order centred round the Throne of God, which Christ came to embody, and so to authenticate afresh in men's convictions. This is one of its main and fundamental characteristics, that every agent has his own place in it, a special talent committed to him, a peculiar and personal ministry into which 'he has been called.' And most plainly did Christ set forth this characteristic by His fulfilment of the lowliest tasks and duties that belonged to His position during the period of which we are thinking, just as He set it forth afterwards in His own teaching and in that of the Apostles whom He instructed. All the time he was bending sedulously over His daily toil, industriously handling the tools of Joseph's craft, and steadfastly accomplishing all the other works belonging to His time and His position—He gloriously reflected that law of the Divine Economy which requires every man to labour in the place and manner which has been ordained by God, and then to leave the results of his diligence to be inwrought by its Ordainer into the great movements of His kingdom, remembering that its advancement and prosperity depend on Him and not upon ourselves.[4]

margin: CHAP. III.
1 Cor. vii. 20.
Rom. viii. 28.
Heb. xii. 27, 28.

In this spirit, and in the practice of these habits, He lived through all those years wherein the youth-

---

[4] The chief disclosures of the unseen world, as we find them in the visions of Micaiah, of Isaiah and Ezekiel, and in the Apocalypse of St. John, strikingly represent that 'functional service, as in a camp of living forces where authority is paramount,' which Christ so marvellously exemplified—as being the universal law of spiritual

F

ful energies of His human nature were restlessly craving another outlet, and while He was wrought upon by influences through which that restlessness was heightened. There, for example, was Herod's court full in view from Nazareth, with all its suggestions of treachery and corruption demanding to be righteously exposed, and put to shame and punished. In that one of 'the king's houses' He could daily see where His unfaithful countrymen, 'gorgeously apparelled,' and 'living delicately,' were prospering on the wages of their perfidy. Nearer home, too, under His closest observation, He witnessed spectacles of baseness and disorder and misrule, of hollowness and insincerity, and of fearful wrong and wretchedness as the result— spectacles that might have carried Him far aside from His quiet but appointed path under the most specious pleas of patriotism and benevolence. Nevertheless He still went on, doing the 'works that were there prepared for Him to walk in.' Still He patiently 'refrained His spirit, and kept it low,'

Marginal references: Luke vii. 25. Psalm cxxxi. John ii. 4. vii. 6. Ephes. ii. 10.

existence. With veiled faces, denoting 'the absence, in spirits that are perfect, of all wish to display their own attractions, their willingness to go anywhere, to do any errands' of duty and love, the inhabitants of the unfallen world are represented in the very same active obedience to the will of God which He so perfectly manifested during the years of which we are here thinking.

until what He called 'His hour,' with its proper claims of duty, had arrived.   CHAP. III.

Year after year, in the very likeness of what are regarded now as dreary lives, was He thus quietly, sedulously occupied with dull, monotonous work which had nothing to commend it except the claims of duty and of faithfulness. And He steadfastly adhered to His purpose, notwithstanding all inducements to abandon it. Amidst the most trying intercourse with uncongenial companions through all those years, He 'did not His own will, but the will of the Father Who had sent Him,' sustained throughout by the principle which He expressed, with reference to this, as to the after-part of His course, in those memorable words, 'Wist ye not that I must be about my Father's business.' 'I have a baptism to be baptised with, and how am I straitened till it is accomplished.'   *Appendix*, Note E.

John v. 30; vi. 38.

Luke xii. 50.

With this view, however, of His 'functional service,' as man amongst mankind, regarding Himself as having been stationed in an appointed place amongst the armies of the 'Lord of hosts,' and realising His corporate existence in this largest sphere of it—we must not associate aught of gloom and weariness. None of the moroseness, the sullenly hard persistence, which we   Matt. xi. 19.

sometimes recognise in such cases, could be discerned in His steadfast perseverance in His work during His years in Nazareth, any more than it was seen in the labours of His public ministry afterwards. The supposition that He ever manifested any spirit of that kind is indeed expressly negatived by that mention of the 'favour with man,' in which He habitually grew. Nor, indeed, could such a demeanour in any wise co-exist with that true view of His corporate Life which we know He entertained from the beginning, and which, all through His course, must always have given animation and ennoblement to His discharge of its most ordinary duties. For He wrought at them in view of the whole Economy into which they entered, and that Whole reflected its glory on the humblest details in which they called Him to engage. As the Servant of God He then felt, and in this character He showed, that every one who duly accepts his place, even though it be a lowly place, in the vast system of existence, becomes so identified with that system, that we may say he has a property in all its greatness and renown. Just as each limb and member has its share in the honour of the body, and as every individual who takes office in a society that is perfectly compacted, enjoys all its credit and distinction, so—as He then showed—so is it with the man who faithfully occupies his appointed place in the great system of existence, 'All things are his, whether the world, or life, or death, or things present, or things to come.' In His human character, Christ habitually realised this truth. Amidst His dreariest tasks and occupations, He was inspired by the knowledge that notwithstanding, yea, rather because of, His form of a servant in God's Kingdom, He was, since He served loyally, even then sharing in all its glory and magnificence. He knew too that this share was duly rendered to Him by all the wise and good who then looked upon His work, just as the sincerest reverence and the lowliest homage of all holy beings is ever awaiting the humblest men who are intent on filling out their appointed place, and who are there accomplishing the good works that have been 'prepared for them to walk in.'

Moreover, He was further animated by the knowledge that all those forces of the universe which harmoniously converged on Him in that place, were there working with His own. Just as each limb, which is labouring in the whole body's service, and which obeys the laws of its activity, is

marginalia: CHAP. III. — 1 Cor. iii. 22. — Rom. viii. 28.

helped by the remainder, and fortified by their entire life and strength; so, as He then showed, is everyone upheld who occupies his true place in God's Kingdom, and who is working there with an eye that is directed simply and sincerely towards the things which are given him to do. In and through the very nature of his position, all the forces of the universe are working together with his own, and He Who controls them all, is on the side of one who thus appears in the form, and thus occupies his position as a servant.

In other words, Christ then knew, and He ever wrought under the power of the knowledge, that 'all things,' the security and welfare of the entire system in the midst of which He was labouring so faithfully, were vitally concerned in His success. And, therefore, there was overcoming strength, though there was never anything like convulsive effort, seen in His exertions. Throughout them, and amidst all the disturbances which they brought on Him, there was the deepest peace at the centre of His Being, as there must be in the consciousness of everyone who is moving in his ordained path around the throne of God. By His mighty energy, along with His unbroken calmness, He showed that, by the very constitution of the Realm which is centred round that Throne, victorious strength, along with the profoundest rest and peace, distinguishes the experience of the man who is serving loyally therein. The eye of such a one is always clear, and his nerve is always 'to true occasions true,' and his heart, even when wrought on most mightily, must be always steadfast and serene.

Isaiah xxxii. 17. James iii. 18.

Here was the secret of His blessedness during those long years, when, with this estimate of His engagements, and thus supported amongst all dulness and weariness in fulfilling them—He came through the household into the community, and took His appointed place, and was recognised amongst its citizens. And thus was man's entire life up to this point afresh revealed by Him in its true form, and its laws again enjoined on our observance. In the dreariest circumstances that can be thought of, He held to that Revealing Purpose under the power of the views which we have unfolded, and thus He showed, more fully than it could in any other manner have been witnessed, the Life which is the guiding and animating 'Light of men.'

CHAPTER IV.

NAZARETH LIFE IN THE NATION.

AND yet His life in that sphere, however completely and faithfully it was occupied, would have been imperfect, maimed and incomplete, had it not passed into still wider developments. There was another Order in which His faculties and affections needed to be exercised; and this Order embraces communities, as each community rises out of, and is organically connected with, its constituent families.

The encompassing Sphere and Order of which we are here speaking, is the Nation. It may be defined as the aggregate of communities which are existing within clearly marked and recognised territorial boundaries, and which are united by common qualities of race and temperament, by ancestral history, and by general interests and sympathies. In this enlarged range and form of existence, the Purposes of His Incarnation—which,

Gen. x. 32.
Deut.
xxxii. 8.

let us once more remind ourselves, were to embody, and, by embodying, to reveal and afresh authenticate the true form of human being—made it necessary that He should also live. For we must recognise the National relation as part of the Divine Economy of life; as an essential constituent of the framework through which God's design in the creation of immortal beings has been accomplished. In this Economy nations grow out of communities through a necessary enlargement, and by the working of the same principle of mutual compensation and helpfulness as that which developes communities from families. The supply of common needs, the satisfaction of individual wants, the growth of the Body by that 'which every joint supplieth,' the fulfilment of deeply seated affections, desires, aspirations—are provided for by National Societies. We may say, indeed, that they furnish an Organ which is not only needed for the supply of many of the necessities of moral natures, but which is also essential to their effective exercise and their plenary development.

From the nature of its constitution, the Nation may be thus confidently spoken of as one of those normal aboriginal forms of common life which are found everywhere throughout the Realm into which

Margin notes: CHAP. IV. — Rev. xxi. 24, 26; xxii. 2. — Ephes. iv. 16.

men have been restored. And, accordingly, it is clearly discerned in those revealing visions of the Celestial World, wherein we read of its 'thrones and dominions,' its 'principalities and powers.' These words, and their connected symbols, would be meaningless and misleading, unless such communities are existing in that upper sphere; unless the Nation is indeed part of that 'pattern of things in the heavens,' after which the human economy of life which Christ came to manifest afresh, has been framed and modelled.

How perfectly this pattern was copied in the Hebrew polity is apparent in almost every page of the Old Testament. Throughout its history and poetry, references to the national life of the Jewish people, as the very ground of their earthly existence, are constantly occurring. The discharge of every obligation connected with this life was made incumbent, without any distinction, on all the members of the commonwealth. The constitution, the very designation, of their tribes; the law which compelled every Hebrew to enrol himself in the national militia; the dependence of the local on the general and supreme courts of judicature; the obligation which required every one of the people to attend the public festivals—made it absolutely necessary that they should all realise their position and character as members of the nation, and recognise the claims and obligations which were therewith connected.¹ Moreover, this consciousness was deepened by the belief, which was never relinquished by the people, even in the darkest seasons of their history, that, as a nation, they were entrusted with a charge which had most important bearings on the welfare of mankind. The same sense of their position and responsibilities was emphatically recognised and dwelt on in the Psalms, which were in popular use throughout all periods of the Jewish history; and it was the ground of the most frequent and urgent prophetic admonitions. Precepts, warnings, rebukes, addressed to the people in their national character, were constantly uttered by their seers and teachers, and were always listened to in the same spirit as

Gen. xviii. 18. Isaiah lx. 3.

---

¹ Dean Milman (*Hist. of Jews*, vol. i. p. 405) has some striking remarks on what he calls the 'unextinguishable nationality' of the Jews in comparison with the comparatively languid and *destructible* patriotism of other nations, and on the means which have secured the feeling in such energy and permanent vitality. Of those means as they are above enumerated, attendance at the public festivals which compelled them often to meet and travel together in large numbers, and the presence of the Levites, under a secular as well as spiritual character, in every part of the community—were most effective in preserving the people from habits of sullen narrow isolation, and in maintaining a vivid sense of their national interests and relationships.

that which inspired them. So that every Jew, and still more every Jew of the 'house and lineage of David,' must have felt his distinctions as a member of the commonwealth, deeply and indelibly impressed on him. They could not be separated from his habitual consciousness; they constituted the very groundwork of his life; they moulded his existence in the community and in the household. And he must have regarded them too with animation as well as constancy. He must have gloried in his ancestral traditions and his people's history; and, when he remembered Israel's mission in the world, how its typal monarch was to have 'dominion from sea to sea, and from the river unto the ends of the earth,' and how 'all families and kingdoms were to be blessed' in it—he must indeed have 'rejoiced in the gladness of his nation, and gloried in his inheritance.'

Hence, from the nature of the case, we may be certain that this part of the Divine Order was always witnessed in Christ's human character, was therein embodied and reflected, and so proclaimed afresh as binding on mankind. Our remembrance of the Purposes of His Incarnation justifies this statement. And it is further supported by the unquestionable oneness and consistency of the later with the earlier years of His career.

For none of that mere cosmopolitan indifference in which He is sometimes represented—as, for example, by writers who have spoken of ' His great soul rising above all national distinctions,' and of ' His standing forth not as a Jew but as a man '— was ever seen in Him. On the contrary, all through the years of his active ministry, He identified Himself nationally with the people of His birth : He was a Jew in all matters of outward observation and conformity.² It was not to reason or philosophy, but to the fathers of His nation, that He appealed when He was rebuking the degeneracy and corrup-

---

² 'Looking into the documents from which, and not from our "spiritual instincts, and knowledge of character," we can alone learn what Christ really was, we are impressed by this fact, that He stands before us in perfect harmony and keeping with everything around Him. He is not a foreigner ; nor does He wear that cosmopolitan garb with which some would fain invest Him in the scene in which His life was passed. On Jewish ground He was a Jew, and was identified with all the Jewish institutions. Not only is it the countenance of a son of Abraham, with all the Hebrew features marked on it, that we are beholding, but we see that He has adopted the social language and habits of His nation. He has identified himself closely with the people of His birth. He observes their customs, He reverences their authorities, He frequents their assemblies, He worships in their temple, their institutions are supported by His offerings. Again I say, we must not consult our own notions as to what He was, and what He did ; we must take the Evangelists' account of Him ; and now, taking it, tell me of anything which was left undone by Him, through which He could have shown more clearly than He actually did show, that He was a Jew in all matters of outward observation and conformity.'—*Reasons of Faith*, (2nd edit.) pp. 52, 53.

tions of His age. In fact, He 'never showed his Judaism more conspicuously than when He uttered those invectives which have been adduced as reasons for divesting Him of His character as the Son of David, and for removing Him from His place amongst the posterity of Abraham. Every one of those occasions on which He manifested His spiritual nobleness, His own entire freedom from all the unworthiness which we associate with the Judaism of that period—may be alleged in proof that it was a Hebrew countenance which looked with such indignant anger on those corruptions; and that it was in a voice wherein we can recognise the tones of the best Jews in the purest eras, that He so earnestly rebuked them.' Unquestionably, therefore, this was true of Him during His abode at Nazareth. So that in figuring Him there before our minds, we must not only regard Him as the member of a household, discharging all family obligations; and also as the member of a community bearing its burdens, and busying Himself with its responsibilities; we must also think of Him in the character of a patriot, recalling the memories which were so closely associated with those historic scenes around Tabor, and Carmel, and Gilboa, which came constantly within His view.

Reasons of Faith, p. 54.

Appendix, Note B.

The heroic ages and examples of His fatherland; its great mission, so passionately dwelt on by the prophets, and which has yet to be accomplished —filled His human spirit, and constantly formed the animating themes of His discourse, especially when He dwelt on the national degeneracy, and anticipated the lamentations which He afterwards uttered so pathetically as He looked upon Jerusalem.

CHAP. IV.

Matt. xxiii. 37, 39.

Moreover, it should be carefully observed that this aspect of His life was brought out with especial force, and was made signally impressive, by the peculiar circumstances of His people in those years. It is true, indeed, that the national spirit was as strong in them as ever, but their country, as one of the Imperial provinces, was then reduced to an absolute, if we may not say an abject, dependence on the Roman power.

Their position at that time has been well likened to that of British India under our own government. 'The distant British monarch might be named as the parallel of the distant Roman Emperor; the Governor-General occupies a position much resembling that of the President, or Proconsul of Syria; while the Governor of one of the provinces is as the Procurator of Judea. The native princes, the allies and tributaries of the British Government,

Dr. Traill's *Josephus, Introduction*, vol. i. p. 28.

stand in the place of the Herods, the Agrippas, and Philips; the kings and tetrarchs who ruled by the permission, and during the pleasure, of the sovereign foreign power.' Such as these were the political circumstances of Palestine and its inhabitants, at the period under observation; and they were singularly fitted to supply a test which should bring out the spirit and demeanour of the truest, loftiest patriotism.

The characteristic marks of that spirit can be unmistakably ascertained and indicated. It is plain that one who was really possessed by it, would never shrink from taking prompt advantage of every occasion which required a distinct and emphatic assertion of his nation's claims and character. Clear of everything which might have the appearance of unworthy and timeserving compromise, he would earnestly range himself, after the manner of the best among his ancestors, upon his country's side, and insist zealously on its standing and prerogatives; faithfully pointing out, at the same time, the causes of its weakness and degeneracy. On the other hand, he would not less carefully avoid everything like mere fanaticism in that direction; and he would watchfully hold himself aloof from every desperate and frenzied

Nehem. i. 4-11.
Acts xxvi. 4-7.

enterprise which might aim at the recovery of merely outward political independence. Indeed, he would not ascribe any value to such independence, when it could only be obtained and held by stratagem or force, without any regard to the spirit in which such a possession should be treasured, and in an unmindfulness of that moral discipline through which fitness for holding it should be acquired.

Under such circumstances as those in which Christ lived, this would evidently be the course of genuine patriotism. And how perfectly it was fulfilled by Him, may be learned from the expressive silence of the narrative, as well as from its explicit statements in those pages where His words and acts have been recounted in detail.

In all the distinctive habits of His life, and in His most emphatic declarations, especially in His acceptance of the title 'Son of David,' and His frequent allusions to the connection of that generation with the generations which preceded it—we have seen good reason to believe that, in His later years, His national position was formally assumed by Him, that His life throughout was habitually manifested in Hebrew costume and expression. Now all our grounds for this assurance show as

Matt. ix. 27; xxi. 9; xxii. 45.

Supra, p. 78.

plainly that He had zealously assumed this position during the earlier years of His seclusion. Not only does this follow, as we said, from considering the Purpose of His Incarnation, but the fact is necessarily involved in the consistency and oneness of His whole life. We hence gather the strongest assurance that He spoke in Nazareth upon this subject in the tones which He subsequently used; that then also the sentiments, the memories, the hopes, which befit an ardent patriot, were heard from him. Animated and exulting when He dwelt on His ancestral history, He mourned also throughout those earlier years over His people's degeneracy, and inveighed against the blindness and corruptions which were the causes of their deep humiliation. Then, too, He sorrowed with that same grief which He afterwards manifested as He wept over Jerusalem, and the days which He saw were coming on her, through evils which were already causing the land to fester into a carcase, upon which the eagles of retribution must be gathered.

Thus in the years of which we are thinking, did He show His patriotic attachment to His fatherland. And yet, not less markedly, did He then, as afterwards, hold himself aloof from the ungoverned, frenzied movements of the insurgent spirits of His day; nay more, there is good reason to believe that He earnestly discouraged them. It is well known that at that time Galilee was frequently the scene of rebellious outbreaks, against the Roman Government, which were undertaken by men who were desperate and frenzied by oppression, and who were often marked by purest sincerity and noblest zeal, believing themselves fully justified in their endeavours.[3] And yet, while it cannot

[3] 'One of the most serious of these outbreaks, in which all Galilee must have been involved, took place immediately after, and in consequence of the deposition of Archelaus. The increased tribute, which followed on the enrolment that had been made under Cyrenius, was made more odious to the people by the fact that it was farmed by residents in their towns and villages. The "receipt of custom," or tax-office, was in the midst of them: this badge of degradation was constantly in view; and their restless impatience under it, exasperated fiercely the discontent which many already felt on witnessing the gradual heathenising of the province, and shed fresh venom into the ill feeling which existed between them and their Gentile neighbours. Of this feeling the leaders of rebel bands, some of them being fanatics, some mere banditti, eagerly availed themselves, and in one instance with conspicuous success. Judas of Galilee, whether patriot or brigand, "drew away," at this very time, "much people" to follow him. Intrenched in those spacious caves of the ravine which runs up from the Gennesareth plain, that had harboured the robber bands which were driven out by Herod in his youth, it was a long time before they were subdued. But the outbreak, though quelled for the time, disclosed such inquietude and discontent, that larger bodies of troops were draughted into the country. Centurions, with their bands of profligate soldiers, were to be found in every considerable town of the province, such as Capernaum, Nazareth, Cana, and Sepphoris."—*Scripture Lands in connexion with their History*, pp. 283, 284.

indeed be said that He coldly frowned on all those enterprises—for did He not choose one from the very parties who were engaged in them to be numbered amongst the Twelve—yet they never received from Him either assistance or encouragement.⁴ Milton's representation, which declares that, at this time,

> ' Victorious deeds
> Flamed in his heart, heroic acts; one while,
> To rescue Israel from the Roman yoke,
> Then to subdue and quell, o'er all the earth,
> Brute violence and proud tyrannic power '—

is not only unsupported by any authority that can be gathered from the Evangelists, but is quite out of keeping with every account of his demeanour. No: in the very spirit which afterwards led Him to 'depart from those who would have made Him a king,' He constantly refused to take any share in the insurgent movements which then were going forward. From the mere fanaticism of the politicians of those days, He turned habitually and steadfastly away.

In such well-defined occupancy of His national

---

⁴ Simon Zelotes, or the Canaanite. The former of these designations of the Apostle is the Greek equivalent of the latter, which is the one used by Matthew and Mark. Each of these clearly indicates the fact that Simon had belonged to one of those insurgent parties out of which the sect of the Zealots originated.

position, in such a sincere and zealous acceptance of its claims as the ordinance of Him who hath 'divided to every nation its inheritance,' along with a persistent abstinence from all unnatural, premature, and impatient methods of accomplishing its duties—this sphere of life also was perfectly filled out by Him, and authenticated.

CHAP. IV.
Deut. xxxii. 8.

And amidst circumstances that were remarkably fitted for such a disclosure, He then showed, by His words and His demeanour, as one of the Hebrew people, what are the rules and laws of true national existence. They were so embodied in His life as distinctly to make known in what manner they should be observed in every possible combination of events; in what way communities, which are made up of well-ordered families, and which are organically compacted according to the true laws of their association—may, however they are circumstanced, form themselves into nations which shall worthily take a place among the unfallen 'principalities and powers.' Just as He stood forth in this position, should they stand whose fatherland is honourably recognised amongst mankind. And those who are living where it has been depressed beneath its just position, through the unfaithfulness of its sons, may also see how,

Supra, p. 74

without any compromise of duty, they should as patriots demean themselves; as they may hence also learn what are at once the lawful and the most effective methods through which their nation's place and prerogatives may be recovered.

Divine Kingdom, p. 197.

In short, all the courage and self-devotedness, the far-sighted wisdom and noble self-control of genuine patriotism, were witnessed during those thirty years in Nazareth, as they were witnessed afterwards through the scenes of His public ministry in Capernaum and in Jerusalem. What

Rom. xiii. 1.
Titus iii. 1.

the seers and prophets had already declared, and what in later days the Apostles taught to be the will of God in this department of man's social life, was visibly embodied in His own proceedings, in His acts and also in His abstinences; and it was so embodied amidst events than which none can be imagined as better fitted for accomplishing this one of the Purposes of His course as man amongst mankind. We may say that in His national, as in His municipal and household life, the very ideal of existence was beheld in Him.

All the acts in which He discharged these relationships were perfectly blended together in harmonious development, so that the works belonging to each never embarrassed, or interfered with, those belonging to the others. As the three spheres of being, rising one out of the other, make up the beauty and strength of the Economy which is constituted by their union, so was it in His Person and proceedings. The symmetrical completeness of the Whole, as well as the entireness of its several parts, was therein perfectly reflected.

CHAPTER V.

CHURCH LIFE IN NAZARETH.

CHAP. V.

IN surveying Christ's perfect embodiment of the Divine Order as He thus throughout those early years harmoniously blended, in perfect fulfilment, one duty with another, we have, all along, observed His recognition of the relations in which He stood towards God, and towards the communities which are centred round His throne. It was plainly in what the Bible calls a Godly spirit, and under an habitual consciousness of the Divine and Celestial bearings of His earthly Life, that every trial and restraint in it was borne, and that all its active duties were discharged.

Ephes. ii. 19.
Heb. xii. 22.

And this is just saying, in other words, that He thought and spoke, and that He ever acted, as one who knew that this earthly scene of being has been incorporated into the heavenly sphere of purity and love, having been so blended therewith as to form one congruous whole; and that He showed that the perceptions and emotions of that higher sphere should rule men everywhere, through all times and occasions, and in the discharge of every obligation. It was thus that, like the patriarchs of His nation, or, we may rather say, like those unfallen beings who are ever looking towards the throne—He 'walked with God.' 'God was in all His thoughts.' And, as He afterwards declared that, in His human character, as the 'Son of Man,' He was 'in heaven,' while He was still busied amongst the duties, and was carrying the burdens, of His earthly course, so was it in Nazareth, during the years of His seclusion. He lived and moved and had his being there, as one who knew that His Commonwealth was in Heaven. His 'affections were set on things above.' In every development of His personal life, in His household and community, and in His position as a member of the nation, this heavenly character and demeanour were observed in Him.

That calm and noble bearing which distinguished those earlier years befitted one Who knew that, as Man, He was even then living in the 'City of God, the heavenly Jerusalem, amongst an innumerable

CHAP. V.

Gen. v. 24; vi. 19.

John iii. 13.

Philipp. iii. 20.
Coloss. iii. 1, 2.

Heb. xii. 22, 23.

company of angels, and the spirits of just men made perfect.' And, while this consciousness ruled Him at all times, and on every occasion of duty and of trial, it was chiefly shown—its most emphatic expression was witnessed—in His Church Life. It was manifested most clearly in His celebration of the worship, and His observance of the laws and ordinances, which belonged to the Divine Society into which He had been sacramentally admitted.

Divine Kingdom, chap. iii.

This Holy Fellowship had been established in the beginning of the world, as a witness of man's recovery from the loss into which he had brought himself by his apostasy, and also as a means of perfectly delivering him from the effects of it, and re-establishing him in complete oneness with those communities which still abide in their allegiance. For these ends, the Church was added on to the older associations already existing in families and cities, supervening, as by a new creation, upon the aboriginal order of man's being. We are told that every other form of human fellowship was beheld by the Apostle, when the Celestial Economy was revealed to him. Therein he saw communities, with their families and households; and He also beheld the symbols of royalty and dominion. But it is

Revel. xxi. 10, 22, 23.

expressively said that, as he looked through the farspreading scene, he 'saw no temple there.' Unfallen beings have no need either of the instruction or of the help which are furnished by the Institution of which such structures are memorials. In man's circumstances, however, those requirements are urgent. He must be constantly reminded of his relationship towards God, and of his connections with his fellow inheritors of being, especially with those past generations of mankind who are dwelling, during his earthly life, in the region of departed souls. And he requires helps, besides, in warding off evils by which his earthly existence is beset, and in accomplishing those purposes which the deepest instincts of his nature assure him are those for which he was created.

Such are man's urgent needs. And they are effectively provided for in the Church's Society and Institutions. That Society existed at the time of which we are speaking, it was seen, and its intention was expressed—in the Synagogues of Israel, and in the Temple. And we are expressly told that it was 'His custom' then to attend the services of the Synagogue every sabbath day. Thus was His participation in the Church-Life of Israel continually witnessed; and it was also witnessed

CHAP. V.

Divine Kingdom, ubi sup.

Luke iv. 16.

still more impressively by His participation in the temple worship, when, in that obedience to the Mosaic ordinances which we know He habitually practised, He went up, at the appointed seasons, to its more remarkable assemblies and services.

How the Synagogue was constituted, and what forms of worship and instruction were used in it, is as well known as are the particulars of any of the institutions belonging to that period.[1] Its antiquity may be uncertain, but, at all events, we know that it was then found, in every village as well as town, where Jews were living, maintaining the testimony which their people were commissioned to uphold and propagate, and celebrating forms of Divine service which Moses had enjoined on them. Prayers, in liturgical form, and compiled for the most part from the Inspired Writings; readings from the Law and the Prophets; instruction from men who were reputed to have deep insight into truth, along with prophetic exhortations—made up the Synagogue services, as they were then celebrated. Throughout, it was assumed in them that man had been redeemed and restored into God's Family and Kingdom. They declared his union with 'angels

Chap. V.

John vii. 14.

Appendix. Note D.

Vitringa, *On Synagogue.*

---

[1] An account of the arrangements and services of the Synagogue at this time, is given in Note D. of the Appendix.

and archangels and all the company of heaven;' and they also constantly reminded him of his connection with the fathers who were then dwelling in Sheol or Hades, the realm of the departed.[2] Moreover, they expressed the grateful consciousness of men who knew by what a costly price they had been reinstated in God's kingdom, and who acknowledged their relationships therein; and they also expressed contrition for failures in discharging the duties which belonged to those relationships, and asked that strength might be given for their subsequent fulfilment.

Such was the nature of the Synagogue worship, and such were the truths that were conveyed by it. Moreover, in the person of its Elders and Ministers, and of the Council which was formed by them, and which appears to have been at this time

Art. Synagogue, Bib. Dict., and Vitringa, ubi sup.

[2] It is certain (see Vitringa, and Art. Synagogue, *Bib. Dic.*) that there were allusions to the dead in the prayers of the Synagogue. The real nature of these offices of devotion is matter of well-known controversy. But, in any case—whether they were simple acts of communion, or utterances of interceding supplication—they brought past generations distinctly into view before the worshipper, as part of the Society into which he had been incorporated. He lived in the presence of their members. They had a property in him, and he in them. He was consciously joined on to those spirits of the departed. Then, in numbers constantly increasing, they were assembled in Sheol, or Hades, to which in His after discourses Christ frequently alluded, and which must, long before, even during the period which we are here contemplating, have been explicitly recognised by Him.

in relations of dependence on and subjection to the Sanhedrim at Jerusalem—it exercised a control, which was guarded and enforced by the severest penalties, over every part of Jewish life. It influenced, if it did not rule, the existence of the Israelite in his domestic and social, and in his national character; sustaining and purifying every relation which belonged to him. And, as we shall see, there is sufficient reason for believing that to this government of the Synagogue in Nazareth, our Lord was habitually submissive; as it is certain that, by an unbroken custom, He joined in its prayers, and reverently listened to its readings and instructions.

We know, from His own words, what superstitions had gathered round these exercises; and how they had been enfeebled in their celebration and disfigured by habits of thoughtless and even idolatrous formality. Every corruption which has ever spoiled and perverted Divine worship, was seen then in the Synagogue observance of the Hebrew ritual, although it contained, and chiefly in inspired words, some of the noblest proclamations of every ordinance of the Divine Law, and some of the most touching utterances of prayer and thanksgiving that have ever been used in the devotions of the sanctuary. Yet, perverted and misused as this ritual was, He sincerely and habitually worshipped by its means. Unhindered by the dulness and irreverence of those around Him, and looking through the corrupted methods in which these forms of Divine service were celebrated, to the truths which were expressed in them, entering into their spirit, submitting himself meekly to the influences which they were intended to convey—He earnestly employed them all. The Schemah, the Shemonch-Esreh, the Daraschoth were thus used by Him as affirmations of His Divine Calling, and also as channels through which grace was conveyed for its fulfilment.[3] By their means He recognised, and, in recognising, He bore witness to, the facts of man's redeemed position; communing with His Heavenly Father and with all sharers of existence in the use of them, and receiving fresh supplies of strength, and of quickening inspiration, from their testimony and assurances.

[3] The Schemah consisted of three portions selected from the Law, viz., Deut. ix. 4–9; xi. 13–21; Numb. xv. 37–41. The Shemonch-Esreh consisted of eighteen prayers, of which the greater part were said to have been composed by Ezra and his colleagues. And the Daraschoth, derived from the verb signifying 'to enquire into' or 'discuss' (Cf. 1 Cor. i. 20; Titus iii. 9), was the exposition, or sermon, such as that which our Lord Himself afterwards delivered, as recorded by St. Luke (iv. 16).

CHAP. V.

Luke iv. 16.
John xviii. 20.

That very significant allusion by the Evangelists to His customary attendance at the Synagogue, connected with His well-known habits in after years, assures us that, all through that earlier period, He joined in its worship and listened to the instructions which were delivered in its teaching. Nor, still holding to our belief in the consistent oneness of His earthly course, can we doubt that His later recognition of the salutary connections which existed between the Church Institute and common life—as when He spoke of its influence

Matt. xviii. 15 ; xxiii. 2, 3.

in 'reconciling the brother who had trespassed,' and of the injunctions which the 'scribes who sat in Moses' seat' were uttering—had been also manifested throughout His abode in Nazareth. Every Synagogue was meant to carry out the secular laws of Moses ; thus raising the tone of thought and feeling in the families surrounding it, and strengthening the bonds which united their mem-

Reasons of Faith, p. 148.

bers to each other. Purifying, restraining, and ennobling influences were meant to flow out from it, through which the moral and physical welfare of the whole community might be promoted. Nor can we think that of those uses also of the Synagogue, by which, wherever it was found, the Church was represented—He was unmindful. They were neither neglected nor discouraged by His means. On the contrary, both by His own obedience, and by the influence which He exerted—this part also of the Restoring Dispensation was fulfilled by Him.

And, in the same way, with the same spirit and purpose, He went up at the appointed seasons, at Passover and Pentecost, and at the Feast of Ingathering—to take part in the Temple services, to which those of the Synagogue were carefully conformed. That at this time, He went up, not only on the occasion named by the Evangelist, but habitually, to Jerusalem, at the great festivals, will hardly be questioned when we duly consider His position and His purposes. Attendance on those festivals was obligatory on every pious Jew; and the after and fuller details of His life show that, by such men, they were in those years observed, habitually and earnestly. Mingling, then, unobservedly, amongst those faithful worshippers, the 'waiters for Israel's consolation,' the Simeons and Annas of the time, and, among them, with the devout Jews who came as pilgrims to the Holy City from every region of the globe—Christ regularly took part, from the years of His boyhood, in

CHAP. V.

Levit. xxiii. 4, 15, 33.

John xii. 29.
Acts ii. 5.

the impressive ritual which was then celebrated on Moriah. From the very first He manifested that same devoutness, in 'spirit and in truth,' which He afterwards commended. In that scene of the national assemblies, amidst the most stirring memories and associations, He openly recognised, and, in thus recognising, He afresh proclaimed, the facts and the duties of man's redeemed position. He communed there with the fathers of His people, and with the denizens of that heavenly sphere with which our earthly abode is blended. And there, too, He received influences which strengthened and quickened Him in discharging all those obligations which, as Man, He had undertaken to fulfil. Nor can we doubt that, on each recurrence of these consecrated seasons, He felt the 'gladness' of those who said 'We will go up into the House of the Lord. Our feet shall stand within thy gates, O Jerusalem.' He rejoiced with His brethren amidst the impressive services which were celebrated on Mount Zion; and, in that communion with them, He confirmed their submission, along with His own, to the ordinances of the Lord. In His common prayer and thanksgiving with them in the Sanctuary of their fathers, He renewed His energies with theirs for the discharge of all the obligations which in that place were so solemnly urged on their regards.[4]

Then again, besides realizing with signal vividness His Divine and heavenly relationships on those occasions, and gaining eminent supplies of 'grace to help' in their fulfilment, through the influence of the moving associations amidst which the Temple services were celebrated—He also looked upon the Sanctuary on Moriah as a distinguished sign of those national purposes for the promotion of which the Church was likewise instituted. And as, by His own submission, and by His influence, He upheld the Synagogue in its beneficent working among the families of Nazareth, so He regarded 'Mount Zion and her assemblies' as an instrument for raising the spirit of the Nation; for counteracting its errors and corruptions, and joining its members in closer unity; and for helping it to fulfil its mission in the world. He

Isaiah iv. 5.

[4] That at this period Christ regularly celebrated the principal feasts in Jerusalem is implied in the habits of His family—whose rigorous Judaism was betokened by the fact that Mary accompanied Joseph to the Holy City—as well as in His habitual fulfilment of the Mosaic appointments. He was, therefore, familiar with Jerusalem, with its circumstances and spirit, long before His public ministry began. And this fact is assumed by the more thoughtful commentators on the Gospel history (e.g. Lange, 'Life of Christ,' vol. i. p. 416, E.T.), as sinister inferences have also been drawn from it by writers of the rationalist 'persuasion.'

looked reverently towards the 'thrones of judgment in the House of David,' and zealously helped in sustaining their authority among the people. And He cordially joined in those expressions of world-wide philanthropy which the Hebrew anthems were continually uttering. 'Let the nations be glad and sing for joy,' He said, 'for Thou shalt judge the people righteously, and govern the nations upon earth.' He constantly remembered how it had been promised that 'Out of Zion should go forth the law, and the word of the Lord from Jerusalem.' And He always pointed to the Temple as a witness that the descendants of Abraham had been called to stand forth among men as the typal patterns of the race; and that 'all nations' as well as families, were hereafter to be 'blessed' by their teaching and example.

[margin: Psalm cxxii. 5. Psalm lxvii. 4. Micah iv. 2. Gen. xxii. 18. Zech. xiv. 8.]

With these views of its secular, as well as of its spiritual, uses in the Divine Order, He observed the ordinances of the Church, both in the Synagogue and in the Temple. Looking through their disfiguring environments, and the mischievous deadening corruptions that had been brought on them—to their real nature and their original intention, He received the knowledge that is conveyed by them, and the genuine influence which is imparted by

[margin: Matt. xxii. 17.]

their agencies; and He also showed how they bear on the discharge of all personal and family and national obligations.

Reverently contemplating His Life at Nazareth under these aspects, it may indeed be said that the archetypal form of the Church, and the essential purposes of its institution, were therein perfectly reflected. Many of His words and deeds are only intelligible on the supposition that He had always recognised it as a disclosure of the Order in which the Will of God is truly and perfectly embodied, and as a system of divinely instituted agencies for restoring men to perfect conformity with the true standard of their life, and for helping them to practise a perfect obedience to the laws by which all existence is controlled. The supernatural realities of which it testifies—in its declarations respecting the Sovereignty of God, the changeless order of His Universe, the terms on which we hold our place amongst its families and kingdoms, the intercourse into which we are brought with them—and the obligations which hence devolve on us, all these testimonies with the demeanour required by them, were habitually and clearly mirrored in His words and His proceedings. And His acknowledgment of them was especially

Divine Kingdom, p. 201.

manifested by His constant protest against those corruptions by which the Divine Society had been enfeebled and perverted.

For even in those years, while He was thus using the Church's ordinances, He faithfully and zealously protested against the abuses which so misrepresented their character, and weakened their efficiency. It is true, indeed, that during the later period in relation to which His teaching and conduct are fully described by the Evangelists, His denunciations of the Church evils of His time, were—as indeed became the prophetic character which was then assumed by Him—most frequent and emphatic. But we may confidently assume that He did not then first begin to utter them, any more than that He commenced in that after period, an observance of the ordinances which before He had neglected. We have the fullest assurance that, all through His earlier life, He maintained the religious habits which we afterwards see Him practising, as they were subsequently practised by the Apostles under His instruction. And, therefore, it is quite certain that, while He diligently and devoutly used all the 'means of grace that appertained to His Church Life, He must often, even in those earlier years, have lifted up His sometimes sadly and sometimes indignantly protesting voice, against Sadducean cynicism and Pharisaic ostentation. Then, too, He condemned the cold formalism and false sentiment, along with the self-seeking plausibilities, of the mere religionists of that day and generation; while at the same time he denounced, with strongest vehemence, the men whom He saw polluting the Sanctuary with ungodly traffic, and making vile merchandise of its corruptions. Often, too, would He then turn men's thoughts back to the great purposes for which the Church had been instituted, and to the purer simpler days in which those purposes had been faithfully accomplished. He 'shewed the House to the House of Israel, that they might be ashamed of their iniquities.' And 'He helped them to measure the Pattern, that they might keep the whole form thereof, and all the ordinances thereof, and do them.'

In this manner he fulfilled the duties of His Church Life by protest and conflict, as well as in the exercises of worship and contemplation. And while He lived and worked through common days and scenes amidst the glorious light thrown on them from the Sabbath hours and from the devotions of the Sanctuary, He plainly recognised every region of man's existence as incorporated in the Divine Sphere of his being, and as forming part of it. He showed how 'this world may be transfigured and glorified, and the world above substantiated and made ours by their mutual blending' on the commonest occasions, and amongst the dreariest, humblest occupations.

CHAPTER VI.

NAZARETH LIFE IN ITS AFTER DEVELOPMENTS.

THIS view of Christ's Church Life harmoniously blending, and firmly compacting, all the other relationships that were sustained by Him, completes our survey of His earlier embodiment of the Divine Order as it is meant to be manifested amongst men. We now see it in its entireness and its perfection. Steadfastly gazing on Nazareth under all the historical lights which converge on it, instructed by all the means of information that are at our command —the very Ideal of human existence comes forth therein, complete under every aspect in which it can be contemplated.

In that undistinguished position, amidst occupations and companions such as are allotted to the great majority of the human race, we observe every relationship fulfilled, every duty calmly and nobly,

Supra, p. 10.

and yet unobtrusively accomplished, in His household and community, in His nation and in the Church. In His connections with all surrounding persons and occasions, and His heedfulness of every one of their just requirements—the common life of man, in its accustomed scenes, was there consistently and greatly lived. The virtues which had been seen in the best men before His time were but faint gleams of that full-orbed refulgence; and, by all men since then, the glory which was there beheld in Him, has been only dimly, brokenly reflected. Surveyed in relation to all surrounding things, Christ's Life in Nazareth was evolved in complete, harmonious development. And it was also seen resting upon, and growing out of, past times and generations. In all His relationships He was united to, and, so to speak, He came forth from, the general mass of His predecessors upon earth. He inherited their attainments and possessions; their vitality was energising in His person and associations; through innumerable channels, their life affected, moulded and determined, that which He lived there during the years which we have been surveying.

And this sense of His connection with past generations, over and above that in which He stood with the men who were then living with Him upon earth, is necessary to complete our view of His position as a member of the race, so that, in the fullest significance, His disciples may recognise Him, as He is there observed in the years of His seclusion, not only as the Son of Mary and the Son of David, but also as the Son of Man. Now, however, we must connect these years with those which followed in His after history: we must see how His Life in Nazareth fulfilled the intention of all human lives in contributing to man's general progress and advancement. This is necessary, because no one's place is entirely filled out, his life is not beheld in all its significance and practical momentousness, unless this connection with the afterhood of its history, has been witnessed and considered.

CHAP. VI.

Matt. xvi. 13.

We have seen then how certain is the fact that Christ's subsequent three years in Capernaum and Jerusalem cannot be regarded as a beginning of His ministry, but showed rather the continuance and enlargement of that which had already been carried forward, through the thirty years preceding. Then, indeed, His embodiment of the Divine Order was brought out more fully and impressively, because then, 'His hour' having come, He emerged from His retirement to enter on His office as a Prophet in the world. But, excepting His prophetic

John ii. 4; vii. 6.

utterances, and the miraculous works by which they were fittingly accompanied, there was nothing in that later course which the Evangelists have described, that can be justly spoken of as new. It is true that in His teaching through His latter years, He spoke with an authority which He had not before assumed; and that, in His miracles, He then opened out the world unseen, and showed the supreme control which He was exercising over all its regions, as He had never previously done. But, with these exceptions, what was seen in, and what was heard from, Him throughout those years, which had not been heard and seen during the long period by which they were preceded? The highest manifestations of wisdom and beneficence, of tenderness and self-devotion—had been already witnessed in His character; those qualities had been lived out, and they had been spoken forth, and amidst the very scenes through which the Evangelists afterwards conduct Him in their history; in families and households, in streets and market-places, in the Synagogue and in the Temple. In all those places, He had been living that same kind of life which we see Him living afterwards; He had toiled amidst its duties, and in it He

Reasons of Faith, p. 90.

Acts i. 2.
1 John i. 1, 2.

had suffered too from the 'contradiction of sinners against Himself,' from the opposition and revilings of those who looked, impatiently and angrily, upon the goodness, the love and righteousness, which they beheld in Him.

Chap. VI.
Wisdom ii. 15.

It was amidst those trials that He had 'increased' in that wisdom, and acquired that spiritual strength and nobleness, which were displayed so conspicuously in His public ministry, as the Evangelists describe it. There, amidst those sufferings, 'He had learned the obedience' with which His Father's will was afterwards accomplished. The power and calmness, the steadfast patience and long-enduring courage, which those writers have so wondrously depicted, were the natural outcome, in His human spirit, of that discipline through which He had long been passing, and to which He had so lovingly submitted. Indeed, we may here remark it as one of the most impressive among the many Divine congruities of truth which may be discerned in the Gospel History, that His after life is presented by His biographers as coming forth in such natural development from that course which a consideration of the Purposes of His Incarnation, and of the scene of their fulfilment, apart from any reference to His

Hebrews v. 8.

John iv. 34.

subsequent history, would show He had accomplished.[1]

Now in this growth, this slow gradual development of His perfections, Christ exemplified a law of the Divine Order, as truly as He did in fulfilling the many relations in which we have been surveying Him. He thus showed how those germs of excellence which are implanted in the human spirit, are meant to be gradually expanded, during the course of years, by loyally and lovingly discharging the duties, and submitting to the restraints and trials, of the earlier stages of existence. There alone can genuine strength and courage and self-control, an absolute mastery over our faculties, and skill and power in using them—be certainly acquired. In what manner the most effective processes of self-culture may be carried forward, and how

---

[1] In the preceding chapters we have assumed that oneness and uniformity of the later with the earlier course on which we are here commenting, and have used it as one of our three sources of information respecting this part of the Divine Life (see *Introduction*). The accordance of its testimony with that of our other two informants furnishes an 'evidence' which is well worth observing. And this will come out still more impressively, if the other two means of information are used independently. That is to say, the Purpose of the Incarnation, and the scene of its fulfilment, being alone regarded, we should see that first in Nazareth such a Life must have been lived as that which we afterwards witness, in Jerusalem and Capernaum, when its prophetic and miraculous characteristics have been deducted.

spiritual perfection is to be sought for and attained, was surely shown, most clearly and instructively, when He came forth from such plainness and monotony, such utter commonness of life as that was amidst which He was living through that long period, in the perfection of a character before which all men, even the noblest, have bowed, and bowed most humbly in their purest, loftiest moods.

CHAP. VI.

Reasons of Faith, p. 38.

Nor was it only in the growth and development of His personal character, that the Laws of the Divine Order were then revealed by Him. He also showed how genuine influence is exerted, and the essential conditions of acquiring it. Of this we are reminded by the statement that during these years He 'grew in favour, with man' as well as God. We remember that it was after the Life in Nazareth had closed, and in Divine approval of His course therein, that the testimony came: 'This is My beloved Son, in Whom I am well pleased.' And it was then, too, long before He had 'manifested forth His glory,' and while the Life was still quietly going forward, that the conviction was awakened, and grew up in the minds of His earliest disciples, that in Him, complete goodness, the loftiest manifestation of human existence, had been witnessed. It should ever be carefully remembered that they were His near

Matthew iii. 17.

John i. 14; ii. 11.

neighbours, men who had long lived, but a few miles away, in His own district of the land, who first followed Him. From what they personally knew, and had seen of Him, they were led to their belief that, in His Life, the 'Light of men' was witnessed. And living with Him, and getting every day into closer intimacy with His mind and character, they found increasing reasons for their trust, until it grew at length into an overpowering conviction. His quietly consistent and unvarying goodness had at length gained their confidence; and, wisely yielding it, they understood Him more perfectly: the human character which had so grown up in their regards, led them onwards to the Divine aspects of His Person. Recognising the Son of Mary and of David, as being also the Son of Man, they came afterwards to know Him as the Eternal Word, the Son of God. And with only one break in its continuity of growth, this assurance strengthened. Once indeed, in an hour of overwhelming trial, an immense shock was given to their convictions. But they soon recovered from the effects of it, and their trust never afterwards deserted them Baptized with Pentecostal fire, they held it with unquenchable ardour to the end, and all life was henceforth tried by the Life which they had witnessed, as by a standard from which there could be no appeal. In the strength of their faith in Him, they overcame the world, and victoriously accomplished the mission to which they had been appointed.

CHAP. VI.

1 John v. 4.

Moreover, by the influence which they exerted, His course in Nazareth still further exemplified, by embodying, the Divine Order of man's being. In that world-wide manifestation of His glorious character which went forward through their agency, we see one of the most momentous laws of man's existence impressively brought forward, since every partaker of immortal life on earth has thus been appointed to send out, by the instrumentality of those immediately around him, influences that shall reach far beyond his own circle, and by which the welfare of mankind is furthered. Now this law also, was fulfilled in the course which we have been surveying. It so wrought on those whom it immediately affected, that through and from them it passed, like leaven in a mass, or like all-pervading light, over the whole earth. This power of Christ's Divine Example had its origin in the habits of His life throughout the thirty years. And in remembrance of them, as well as of the years which followed, it may be truly

Mark xv. 20.

Acts i. 8.

Gal. vi. 10.

2 Pet. i. 7.

I

said that, 'filling every mould of action, every term of duty and of love, with His own Divine manners, works, and charities—all the conditions of human existence have been raised by the meaning which He has shown to be in them, and the grace which He has put upon them. The world itself is changed; it is no more the same that it was: it has never been the same since He lived in it. The air is charged with heavenly odours, and a kind of celestial consciousness, a sense of other worlds, is wafted on us in its breath. Christ and His all-quickening Life are now in the world, as fixed elements, and will be to the end of time, so that we may say, " Look ye hither, all ye blinded and fallen of mankind! there is a better nature among you; a pure heart, out of some purer world, is come into your prison, and He walks through it with you."'

Thus does He exert an universal influence over men s minds and hearts. In this view of it, also, His dominion over the spirits of men 'extends from sea to sea, and from the river to the ends of the earth.' And this function of His world-wide rule began in Nazareth during the thirty years which we have been reviewing. Indeed, we there see some of the most striking features of this pattern left by Him for universal imitation. Some of the most im-

[margin: CHAP. VI. Bushnell's Nature and the Supernatural, chap. x.]

[margin: Psalm xxii. 8. John xii. 32.]

pressive tones of the voice which is heard in all ages and regions, and through every generation, were uttered there; and just because His place and circumstances, amidst the common paths of men, throughout those early years, brought Him into closer relations with the majority of those who continually look to Him for teaching and example. Moreover, by means of what we there witness, we can better understand the after life which His biographers have written in detail: we can enter, more intelligently, and with deeper interest, into the meaning of the lessons which He taught, by word and deed, during the years of His public ministry, in Capernaum and in Jerusalem.

Heb. ii. 7.

Luke xxiv. 19.

Nor may we here omit to notice that His pattern in that earlier part of His course becomes more imitable, as well as more intelligible, by the power of His sympathy. For eminently there we may realize His fellowship, and feel the power of His Redeeming Love, while we copy His example. Here, however, and in looking towards this aspect of our subject, the profoundest reverence is needed, and we must be careful not to contravene, by any of our own words respecting it, the utterances of the Fatherly and Prophetic instructors of the Church.

CHAP. VI.

And yet, heedfully bearing in mind their teaching concerning the highest ends of His Incarnation and Atonement, we cannot speak of His course throughout that earlier period—when, in every relation which then devolved on Him, He 'did not His own will, but the will of the Father who sent Him,' when His constant rule of conduct was, 'Not my will, O God, but Thine be done'—except as part of the manifestation of that Divine Sacrifice through which our world has been restored to its place in the Divine Kingdom. His Life in Nazareth, with its severe restraints and its bitter trials, arose from, and it disclosed, that law of self-devotion which holds good universally, on which the safety and welfare of the universe is based, and of which the highest illustration has been witnessed in that Atoning Work through which man's redemption was secured. It was joined on to the self-denials and sorrows of His after years, to the 'agony and passion' which ended in the 'precious death' wherein that illustrious Work was perfected. Did not His Divine Sacrifice begin to be offered up in the very hour of His Incarnation, and was it not carried forward all through His earthly Life unto the end![2] And,

Luke xxii. 42.
John v. 30.

Ephes i. 10.
1 Pet. iii. 18.

---

[2] 'Not only in "His agony and bloody sweat, and in His cross and passion," but throughout the Whole Life of which His last sufferings

thinking now of that earlier part of it, we know that there must have been many hours and days and years, while it proceeded, which wore at least as dark a colouring as any that followed, which were as gloomy and severe. Was His human course indeed sadder and more painful to Him in Capernaum and in Jerusalem, than it had been in Nazareth? Was He not there too a 'man of sorrows and acquainted with grief'? Had not the same inflictions of human malice and perversity, the scorn, the contradiction, the hatred, which pained Him afterwards, already been encountered amidst the hard conditions, the dull and low companionship, by which His Life was there distinguished. Surely through the sufferings which He then endured, and which appeal to every man's experience, He works not

<small>Isaiah liii. 3.
John xv. 18.
Acts iii. 4.</small>

<small>were the climax and consummation, the law of self-devotion was declared by Him. Our popular phrases and modes of speaking on this subject, have obscured the constancy, as well as the naturalness, with which Christ exemplified this obligation. May we not say that our doctrines of justification have veiled from us the Justifier, and that our theories of the Atonement have hidden the sacrificial Life and Death of Him by whom it was effected? Moreover, the symbols, as well as the dogmas in which they are expressed, have also darkened those realities. It is in deepest reverence and tenderness that I would here ask, if our familiar mention of His Cross, and of His Blood, and our often sentimental, and, I must add, sensuous exhibitions of the mere physical sufferings of our Redeemer in the last moments of His life, have not obscured that life-long devotion of His will and affections, in which He "gave us an example that we should follow in His steps."'—*Church Restoration*, p. 149.</small>

CHAP. VI.

less powerfully than by His sufferings afterwards upon our minds and hearts, and then too He clearly showed forth the law through which all deeds that are being wrought for man's true welfare must be accomplished. Every benefactor of our race will see that in doing his work effectively, he must be a 'partaker of Christ's sufferings' in Nazareth, as well as in Jerusalem; and must become 'conformed to the death' in which there, too, He died to sin, and lived the true life of man towards God.

Rom. vi. 10. Gal. ii. 20, v. 24. Philippians, iii. 10.

We thus realize, and are strengthened by, His sympathy, while we are instructed by His teaching. When in this manner we see Him 'compassed about with our most ordinary 'infirmities,' and 'in all,' even in the commonest things, 'made like unto His brethren, while yet He was without sin'—we approach Him, not only with deeper reverence, but with more brotherly regard. From that perfected sense of His oneness and fellowship with men, special grace is given in our commonest 'times of need,' 'grace to help' in the long drawn-out and saddened dreariness which must always make up the largest portion of every earthly life which is truly passed according to His will.

CHAPTER VII.

CONCLUDING APPLICATION.

THAT perfection in which we now behold Him, and in which He justified every faithful true-hearted man who preceded Him on earth, besides strengthening and instructing all who follow—comprises many parts and aspects, and some of these have special uses and significance in different regions and periods of the world's history. Nor can any thoughtful 'observer of the times' question that the portion of the Divine Life on which we have been dwelling, has peculiar bearings of this kind upon our own day and generation.

In Bishop Butler's words, if we may again use them with this reference—'Events,' now happening, 'open out and ascertain' this part of the Inspired Record, for in this character we may regard it, although the facts therein contained have not been explicitly related. Every one who has

Analogy, pt. ii. chap. iii.

gone in spirit to Nazareth, and who has attentively watched that plain and quietly ordered, but at the same time strong and noble Life which was lived there, and who has then called to his remembrance the circumstances amidst which changed fashions and modes of being have now brought mankind—must feel that those thirty years utter a special voice to ourselves. And this fitness of theirs for our 'teaching and rebuke,' and for our 'instruction in righteousness,' appears more striking when we consider certain moral influences, which are working, along with obvious physical causes, to produce the evils which are at once the theme, the perplexity and the despair, of every thoughtful watcher of the times. The impatient haste, the self-willed 'devices and desires,' to which we are now referring, and which, added on to the constant evils whereby man is afflicted — furnish the special distinctions of our age, largely arise from those heightened sensibilities which the Christian Revelation has produced in the hearts of men who have looked only partially upon the facts which it discloses, or who have never conversed with these facts at all, except through the intercepting veil of the symbols by which they are represented. Christ's Gospel has raised such men's standard of life and duty, but it has not yet brought clearly into their view those truths and motives which would at once supply the genuine overcoming strength through which the requirements of that standard might be fulfilled.[1] Their sense of moral obligation has been heightened, but it has been only by an incomplete perception of realities which, seen in their entireness, would at once explain the 'unhasting, and yet unresting,' fidelity and steadfastness with which Christ accomplished His work during that most trying period of His earthly course, and which is in such marked contrast with the unbelieving impatience and eagerness of our day and generation.

CHAP. VII.

Ephes. iii. 18.

Isaiah xxviii. 16.
Luke xxi. 19.

[1] It has been well observed by a thoughtful and acute writer, that 'Christianity has indeed spread in late years, superficially, but it has not spread deeply. Everywhere it has been raising the tone of moral sentiment, purifying the domestic atmosphere, removing from view throughout Christian countries whatever is morally offensive, cherishing and promoting beneficent enterprises, bringing all minds into a habit of kindly reflectiveness. Yet it has been making little or no progress as a deep spiritual power. It has not evolved,' i.e. by means of its disclosures of revealed facts, 'mighty influences within the bosoms of men individually. And the consequence of (such) a diffusion of Christianity under this aspect of a mild, purifying, but powerless influence, must,' he adds, 'be an antagonistic reaction from Christianised sensibilities upon Christianity itself,' through the influence, i.e. of the tempers which have thus been originated by means of facts that are only partially apprehended, and which must be seen in their entireness, in order to satisfy the standard which they have been the instrument of establishing.

This contrast becomes more impressive the longer we dwell on it, and reflect upon the causes by which it has been produced. And it furnishes many obvious and valuable lessons, to some of which, in conclusion, the reader's attention is here specially directed.

The chief of these lessons has, in part, already been brought forward, when we were observing Christ's work as a member of the Nazareth community, in connection with that which we have all along recognised as the great distinction of His life. Let it be again said that this was not the fulfilment of any 'plan' which He had Himself devised, but rather the embodiment of the aboriginal purpose of all existence, the fulfilment of His Father's Will, and this was to be accomplished by means of the 'good works' which, in that time and place of His Incarnate Life, had been 'prepared for Him to walk in.' Thus living, labouring, and also suffering, we saw that He observed that rule of functional service which is observed by every being who has 'kept the first estate' in which he was created. Nor was it sadly or morosely that He was thus engaged on what the 'world' of His age would think and speak of as His dreary tasks. He wrought upon them cheerfully, in full view of

Marginalia: CHAP. VII. Preface. 1 John ii. 16.

CONCLUDING APPLICATION.

the whole scheme and economy into which they enter, and in the fullest assurance that its purposes would be successfully accomplished. And yet, as we saw, every pretext which seemed fitted to call Him off from those quiet toils, there pressed itself on His attention. Throughout those drearily protracted years, every one of the evils with which afterwards, when 'His hour had come,' He so valiantly contended, were before and around Him, 'provoking indignation, crying aloud for interference. The hollowness of social life; the misinterpretation of Scripture; forms of worship and of phraseology which were hiding truth; injustice, priestcraft, cowardice, hypocrisy'—every mischief which seemed to justify His hasty relinquishment of the work which was set Him, that He might enter on some other, appeared to cry aloud for His protest and resistance. But He never listened to those plausible, but misleading invitations. He went forward steadfastly in His appointed way. The vision which, we may say, had raised His human perception of duty, and which heightened His conscientiousness so loftily, also showed the reasons of His employment in their true form and character, and widely opened out the scenes in which it was carried forward,

CHAP. VII.

Supra, p. 69.

F. W. Robertson's *Sermons*, vol. iii.

Supra, p. 70.

and the associates with whom He was engaged in its fulfilment. And therefore He steadfastly persevered in the very spirit that was expressed in the remarkable words with which He afterwards followed His declaration, 'The harvest truly is great, but the labourers are few.' Those words were not, 'Go ye, yourselves, at once into the harvest field. Step forward wherever you see that the sheaves are ripening for the reaper's toil;' but, 'Pray ye the Lord of the harvest that He will send forth labourers,' whom He hath Himself called and qualified for His own work, and who will do it in the use of those means of utterance and activity which He hath furnished, as each one of them sends up his prayer, 'Lord, what wilt Thou have me to do,' under the power of an inspiring desire to labour in His cause.

That loyal adherence to appointed duty, in its rebuking contrast with the self-asserting spirit which, more or less, has marked every age—nobly vindicated all sincere though often decried and misapprehended labourers in earlier days, and it stands forth as an illustrious example of steadfastness in discharging the most trying and wearisome obligations through all time to come.

In every generation it has thus been profitable

for teaching and rebuke. But, as we said, it addresses specially emphatic admonitions to ourselves. How severely, for example, does it bear on those bustling philanthropists, those 'doers of good' amongst us, whose 'doings' have such a suggestive resemblance to the world's vanity and restlessness. Amidst the pleasant excitement of their publicities, they are professedly furthering Christ's cause, and they freely use His name to sanction their endeavours; yet we can hardly imagine any stronger contrast than is seen when we compare that long portion of His Life with theirs, and His methods then of doing His Father's Will with those which they are using! Surely His desire was at that time as earnest as ever for the promotion of man's welfare, and He was then as impatient as He ever felt with the evils which were hindering it. Yet he waited and worked on in His appointed sphere, until 'His hour' had come, or, in other words, until He was called by God to that work of protest and of resistance, for which our modern philanthropy requires no summons but its own emotions and impatience.

Impressive lessons of most seasonable rebuke may well be drawn from those thirty years in this view of them. And then how gloriously do they *Church Restoration, ad finem.*

vindicate the course of others who are grievously suffering through that plausible and busy restlessness, and whose perplexities and discouragements it is increasing. Those martyr toilers and sufferers who are abiding in so many hidden places throughout the land, as each one patiently 'waits for Israel's consolation,' and 'refrains his spirit, and keeps it low,' amidst his labours and his self-denials—may well look triumphantly towards that lowly scene, where Christ's Life was going forward in the very image of their own. Day after day did He work and suffer there, amidst weary loneliness, and aching lack of sympathy, just as they work and suffer now who are waiting on their sad and heavy ministries, uncheered and unrequited. Joy and triumph surely to all these sons and daughters of affliction, when they remember Whose course is reflected in their own, since just like them did He live on, through weary saddened dreariness, in the home and workshop of the carpenter, and amidst the dull ungenial companionship of those long years of His seclusion!

Nor is this all. For that same Living Redeemer, Who when 'He stands in the latter day upon the earth,' will vindicate, as wise and illustrious, the course of so many whose lives 'were accounted

madness and their end without honour'—may even
now be recognised as deeply sympathising with
them in this very aspect of their trial. They may
well remember, and take great comfort from the
recollection, that, as 'in all points' so especially
in this, 'He was tempted' like as they are; and
that 'with the infirmities' which their peculiar trial
specially reveals to them, He has 'a fellow feeling.'
In the unquestionable fact that, long before The
Temptation, He had been often moved to anticipate the season and opportunity which had not
yet arrived, we see a peculiar application of His
sympathy in succouring all who in their uncheered
sadness are in like manner tempted to relinquish
their discouraged and unrequited efforts, and step
forth from overshadowed paths of toil, into the
crowded, sunny highways of the world. And most
thankfully, even in the gloomiest passages of their
lives, may those lonely witnesses and sufferers,
comfort themselves with the remembrance: *By His
experience through those years in Nazareth, He can
feel with us, as well as for us, in these sad days,
amidst these apparently frustrated efforts, and fruitless toil, and while this unheeded testimony is being
borne. In that weary time, He suffered what we are
suffering now. And, on the ground of this common*

CHAP. VII.

Heb. ii. 17, 18; iv. 15, 16.

CHAP. VII.

feeling and experience, we can plead before Him with a confidence which otherwise we could not have felt, for His grace to help in this our time of need.

Appendix, Note E.

In its fitness to supply such aid and consolation, as well as in its rebuking contrast with the spirit and habits of the age, we see this neglected part of Christ's history 'spread out, and its meaning ascertained.' And now, as its main features have been brought within our view, if we carefully set that long period of the Divine Life beside those needs of men, which exist indeed in every age, but which are specially urgent in our own—it will come forth still more distinctly and impressively. Every distinction and movement, all the characteristic habits, of the thirty years, will then be clearly manifested. And the Life which is indeed the Light of Men, their Light in every path and in all circumstances of their lives, will be beheld complete in all its aspects. All 'sorts and conditions' of human being, man's estate in every one of its developments, will be therein witnessed in perfectly accurate reflection. Clearly and plainly will this be seen. And seeing it, the question may here well be asked, Can we entertain any doubt by Whom that disclosure was effected?

John i. 49; iv. 42.

Are we not, like those who first witnessed it, now

led from the human character of Christ to the Divine?

Surely we must feel that only the Eternal Word 'Who was with the Father in the beginning,' by Whom the worlds, and the Order which they sustain and manifest, were called into existence—could thus have perfectly embodied and declared the Divine Mind and Purposes. And so it is that we arise from this contemplation of His Human Life, which we now see in its entireness, saying, with a conviction even firmer than we can have ever felt before, 'Jesus of Nazareth, Thou art none other than the Son of God;' as with our completer apprehension of the benignant work which He has thus so perfectly accomplished, we must then add, with profounder and more grateful reverence than ever, and of a truth, 'Thou art the Saviour of the World.'

APPENDIX.

CONTENTS.

NOTE A. *Reasons for the Silence of the Evangelists respecting the Events of the Thirty Years* . . . 131

NOTE B. *Nazareth and its Neighbourhood* . . 133

NOTE C. *On Jesus increasing in Wisdom* . . 137

NOTE D. *On the Synagogue and its Worship* . 139

NOTE E. *Practical Lessons* 141

APPENDIX.

Note A.

Reasons for the Silence of the Evangelists respecting the Events of the Thirty Years.

In F. Spanheim's '*Dubia Evangelica*' (xcvi. Pars II. pp. 650–3) will be found a careful treatment of the questions, *Cur tantum διάστημα Historiæ Evangelicæ reperiatur apud Matthæum? Et cur acta pueritiæ, adolescentiæ, et juventutis Christi silentio transmissa ab omnibus Evangelistis?* After dwelling on the importance of the subject, he presents his views (which fairly represent those which are commonly held) of it, under these five heads; viz.:

(1) Hæc facta per singularem Dei dispensationem, quæ summa ratio est. . . . Dispensat Ille tempora et memoriam temporum pro arbitrio, et sapienter id factum a nobis credi debet. (2) Addi potest, id ipsum non tantum Dei dispensatione factum, sed et convenientissime factum, ut liqueret, Christum nobis per omnia similem

APP. ætatis inferioris infirmitates... suscepisse, et sensim adolevisse, quod notat diserte Scriptura (Luc. ii. 40, 52). (3) Adde sic ostensum, præparatione, et diuturnâ quidem opus esse ad munus in Dei domo convenienter administrandum.... (4) Adde, sapienter a Christo exspectatum tempus, quo cum authoritate doceret, quod nonnisi illorum est, qui ætatem maturam attigêre. (5) Immo illa ipsa dispensatione per συγκατάβασιν singularem Judæorum consuetudo observata, quibus ætas xxx. annorum vel præcepti divini, vel veteris instituti obtentu præfixa, priusquam Docturæ insignibus *clave cum pugillaribus* donarentur, et ad publicum docendi munus admitterentur. Unde (1 Paral. xxiii. 3) ubi Levitarum numeribus initur, illorum tantum capita putantur qui vel triginta annos attigerant, vel illos erant supergressi. Quod ad quævis munera sacra a Judæis promiscue relatum.

For the best account of the Apocryphal Gospels, which profess to supply the omission of the Evangelists, the reader is referred to 'Cambridge Essays,' 1856, and to B. H. Cowper's 'Apocryphal Gospels, with Notes, &c.' London, 1867.

Note B.

Nazareth and its Neighbourhood.

'The city lies on the western side of a long, narrow, basin-like valley, running from N.N.E. to S.S.W. Its houses stand in the lower part of the western slope, which is steep, and rises high above them. This hill is covered with aromatic herbs and flowers; at the very top stands a wely, called Neby Ismail. This lies, according to Robinson, four or five hundred feet above the valley, which itself is not far from a thousand feet above the level of the sea; the measurements vary. The mountains which lie N. and N.W. of Nazareth, are from 1,200 to 1,300 feet high. The loftiest lie N.W.; those less elevated more to the N., they sink towards the E. and S.E., till they rise suddenly again in Tabor. Towards the S.E. the valley of Nazareth becomes narrower, and ends in a winding path leading to the plain of Esdraelon. There are also roads leading east to Tabor and Tiberias, south-east to Jerim, south-west, by way of Cafa and the plain, to Carmel, north-east to Kafirkenna, and north-west to Sefurieh and northern Galilee.

'Both of the latter run E. of the Wely Neby Ismail, whence a magnificent panoramic view may be taken, embracing the beautiful cone of Tabor, Little Hermon, and Gilboa in the east; the mountains of Samaria at the west; the whole plain of Esdraelon, the battle-field of ancient and modern times, is at its foot. Beyond the plain can be seen the long wooded Carmel ridge, reaching to the new convent, and to Haifa, washed by the sea. The city Acca lies hid behind the hills. Toward the north there stretches away another of the beautiful plains that adorn this part of Palestine, El Buttauf, which runs E. and W., and sends its waters into the Kishon. On the northern limit, lies the large village of Sefurieh (Diocæsarea), near to the foot of a solitary peak, on which stand the ruins of a castle. Beyond the plain of El Buttauf, there are long ridges running E. and W., and advancing in height till the mountain of Safed (the city set on a hill, Matt. v. 14) is reached. Farther eastward, lies an ocean of larger and smaller peaks, beyond which the higher ones in Hauran are discernible; and northeast the majestic Hermon, with its cap of snow, is in full view. South-west, but far nearer, the noble promontory of Carmel projects into the silver mirror of the Mediterranean. In the south-east, one standing on the heights in the rear of Nazareth, can see the nature of the country which connects Carmel with the mountains of Samaria; that it consists of a large number of low wooded hills, separating the Esdraelon plain from the fertile valleys at the south of Samaria.

'The same supply of woods and low bushes gives the Carmel range an attractive appearance, remarkably in contrast with the naked hills of Judæa. The beauty and grandeur of the view from the Wely Neby Ismail, together with the almost infinite number of recollections connected with localities in view, make this prospect one of the most sublime and most deeply interesting that the world affords.'—Ritter's *Comp. Geog. of Palestine*, vol. iv. E. T.

'These are the natural features which for nearly thirty years met the almost daily view of Him who "increased in wisdom and stature" within this beautiful seclusion. It is the seclusion which constitutes its peculiarity, and its fitness for these scenes of the Gospel history. Unknown and unnamed in the Old Testament, Nazareth first appears as the retired abode of the humble carpenter. Its separation may be the ground, as it certainly is an illustration, of the Evangelist's play on the word " He shall be called a Nazarene." Its wild character, high up in the Galilean hills, may account both for the roughness of its population, unable to appreciate their own Prophet, and for the evil reputation which it had acquired even in the neighbouring villages, one of whose inhabitants, Nathaniel of Cana, said : " Can any good thing come out of Nazareth ? "

'It was not to be expected that any local reminiscences should be preserved of a period so studiously, as it would appear, withdrawn from our knowledge. Two natural features, however, may still be identified, connected—the one by tradition, the other by Gospel narrative—with the events which have made Nazareth immortal. The first is the spring or well in the green open space, at the north-west extremity of the town; a spot well known as the general encampment of such travellers as do not take up their quarters in the Franciscan convent. It is probably this well, which must always have been frequented as it is now, by the women of Nazareth, that in the earliest

local traditions of Palestine figured as the scene of the Angelic Salutation to Mary, as she, after the manner of her country-women, went thither to draw water. The tradition may be groundless; but there can be little question that the locality to which it is attached, exists, and that it must have existed at the time of the alleged scene. —The second is indicated in the Gospel History by one of those slight touches which serve as a testimony to the truth of the description, by nearly approaching, but yet not crossing, the verge of inaccuracy. " They rose," it is said of the infuriated inhabitants, and " cast Him out of the city, and brought him to a brow of the mountain " (ἕως ὀφρύος τοῦ ὄρους) on which the city was built, so as to " cast him down the cliff " (ὥστε κατακρημνίσαι αὐ ὀν). Most readers, probably from these words, imagine a town built on the summit of a mountain, from which summit the intended precipitation was to take place. This, as I have said, is not the situation of Nazareth. Yet, its position is still in accordance with the narrative. It is built " upon," that is, on the side of " a mountain," but the brow ' is not underneath, but over the town, and such a cliff (κρημνός) as is here implied, is to be found; as all modern travellers describe, in the abrupt face of the limestone rock, about thirty or forty feet high, overhanging the Maronite convent, at the south-west corner of the town.'
—Stanley's *Sinai and Palestine*, chap. x.

Note C.

On Jesus increasing in Wisdom.

'When St. Luke tells us that Our Lord "increased in wisdom and stature," we can scarcely doubt that an intellectual development of some kind in Christ's human soul, is indicated. This development, it is implied, corresponded to the growth of His bodily frame. The progress in wisdom was real, and not merely apparent, just as the growth of Christ's Human Body was a real growth. If only an increasing manifestation of knowledge had been meant, it might have been meant also that Christ only manifested increase of stature, while His Human Body did not really grow. But, on the other hand, St. Luke had previously spoken of the child Jesus as being "filled with wisdom," and St. John teaches that, as the Word Incarnate, Jesus was actually "full of truth." St. John means not only that Our Lord was veracious, but that He was fully in possession of objective truth. It is clearly implied that, according to St. John, this "fulness of truth" was an element of that "glory" which the first disciples beheld or contemplated. This statement appears to be incompatible with the supposition that the Human Soul of Jesus, through spiritual contact with which the disciples "beheld" the glory of the Eternal Word, was Itself not "full of truth." St. John's narrative does not admit of our confining this "fulness of truth" to the latter days of Christ's ministry, or to the period which followed His Resurrection.

'There are, then, two representations before us, one suggesting a limitation of knowledge, the other a fulness of knowledge, in the human soul of Christ. In order to harmonize these statements, we need not fall back upon the vulgar rationalistic expedient of supposing that between St. John's representation of Our Lord's Person, and that which is given in the first three Gospels, there is an intrinsic and radical discrepancy. If we take St. John's account together with that of St. Luke, might it not seem that we have here a special instance of that tender condescension by which Our Lord willed to place Himself in a relation of real sympathy with the various experiences of our finite existence? If, by an infused knowledge He was, even as a child, " full of truth," yet, that He might enter with the sympathy of experience into the various conditions of our intellectual life, He would seem to have acquired, by the slow labour of observation and inference, a new mastery over truths which He already, in another sense, possessed. Such a co-existence of growth in knowledge, with a possession of all its ultimate results, would not be without a parallel in ordinary human life. In moral matters, a living example may teach with a new power some law of conduct, the truth of which we have before recognised intuitively. In another field of knowledge, the telescope, or the theodolite, may verify a result of which we have been previously informed by mathematical calculation. We can then conceive that the reality of Our Lord's intellectual development would not necessarily be inconsistent with the simultaneous perfection of His knowledge. As Man, he might have received an infused knowledge of all truth, and yet have taken possession, through experience, and in detail, of that which was latent in His mind, in order to correspond with the intellectual conditions of ordinary human life.'—Canon Liddon's *Bampton Lectures*, Lect. viii.

Note D.

On the Synagogue and its Worship.

'There are certain traditional peculiarities which have doubtless united together by a strong resemblance the Jewish synagogues of all ages and countries. The arrangements for the women's places in a separate gallery, or behind a partition of lattice-work; the desk in the centre, where the Reader, like Ezra in ancient days, from his " pulpit of wood," may " open the book in the sight of all the people . . . and read in the book the law of God distinctly, and give the sense, and cause them to understand the reading;" the carefully closed Ark on the side of the building nearest to Jerusalem, for the preservation of the rolls or manuscripts of the Law; the seats all round the building, whence " the eyes of all them that are in the synagogue " may be " fastened " on him who speaks; the " chief seats," which were appropriated to the " ruler " or " rulers " of the synagogue, according as its organization might be more or less complete, and which were so dear to the hearts of those who professed to be peculiarly learned or peculiarly devout—these are some of the features of a Synagogue, which agree at once with the notices of Scripture, the descriptions in the Talmud, and the practice of modern Judaism.

'The meeting of the congregations in the ancient synagogues may be easily realised, if due allowance be made for the change of custom, by those who have seen the Jews at their worship in the large towns of modern Europe. On their entrance into the building, the four-cornered Tallith was first placed, like a veil, over the head, or, like a scarf, over the shoulders. The prayers were then recited by an officer called the "Angel" or "Apostle" of the Assembly. These prayers were doubtless many of them identically the same with those which are found in the present service-books of the German and Spanish Jews, though their liturgies, in the course of ages, have undergone successive developments, the steps of which are not easily ascertained. It seems that the prayers were sometimes read in the vernacular language of the country, where the synagogue was built; but the Law was always read in Hebrew. The sacred roll of manuscript was handed from the ark to the Reader by the Chazan or "minister;" and then certain portions were read according to a fixed cycle, first from the Law, and then from the Prophets. It is impossible to determine the period when the sections from these two divisions of the Old Testament were arranged, as in use at present; but the same necessity for translation and explanation existed then as now. The Hebrew and English are now printed in parallel columns. Then, the reading of the Hebrew was elucidated by the Targum, or the Septuagint, or followed by a paraphrase in the spoken language of the country. The Reader stood while thus employed, and all the congregation sat down. The manuscript was then rolled up, and returned to the Chazan. Then followed a pause, during which strangers or learned men, who had " any word of consolation," or exhortation, rose, and addressed the meeting. And thus, after a pathetic enumeration of the sufferings of the chosen people, or an allegorical exposition of some dark passage of Holy Writ, the worship was closed with a benediction, and a solemn " Amen." '—Conybeare and Howson's *St. Paul*, chap. vi.

Note E.

Practical Lessons.

'... There are important truths to be learned from the voluntary and long-continued abode of Christ among the poor. For, first, did he not authorise the condition of which He Himself partook? Did He not effectively give His sanction to the natural gradations of society, by Himself dwelling in one of the lowest of those gradations? ... In living as a mechanic with His (reputed) father, did He not give an explicit sanction to the existence, not of abject, but of decent and industrious poverty? Did he not thereby teach us a lesson of civil economy, if the expression may be used, and authorise the existence in our communities of a humble, but not degraded, of a submissive, but not a servile or a suffering class of poor? Now this is a lesson which the poor man may learn with much profit, in days of wild declamation about equality in earthly enjoyments and possessions. Our Lord practically and powerfully, as practically and powerfully as He could, even by Himself dwelling quietly among the poor for thirty years, contradicted these fanatical declaimers; and no poor Christian man can have a better antidote against their foolish and delusive sayings than is presented by that fact—a fact which will furnish the humble follower of Jesus Christ with a strong and satisfactory reason for being contented with his condition in a well-ordered community, even though that condition should approximate closely to the lowest.

'But this long-continued abode of Our Lord with His parents, furnishes this second lesson—That those whose lot is in the midst of poverty, should patiently endure its privations, its necessary privations, and meekly submit to its reproach. Let it be granted that it sorely tries the faith and patience of even a Christian man, to stand by, the toil and careworn spectator of ease and luxury in which he may not participate, of enjoyments which he cannot share; and, while want, and it may be sorer affliction, is in his own home, to look upon the affluence and pleasures, and perhaps submit to the cruel scorn, of men less virtuous and worthy than himself. It is a sore trial; and his is a noble and heroic character, who can, in such circumstances, possess his soul in patience. But, did Christ set no example, and teach no lesson, and furnish no motive, by which that trial may be wisely and well endured? Yes, truly, He did this; and when the poor man, who takes his principles of conduct from the

Gospel, feels rising within himself the strong emotions of impatience and indignation at what he may deem the hard features of his lot, let him think of the seclusion of his Lord for thirty years amid the humility and privations of His father's home, and that for all this time He sat not, though He might have done, at the table of the rich, nor shared in their fascinating pleasures and gay pursuits, but submitted to many wants, and endured, it may be, much contempt. Let the poor man think of this, and he will derive patience and strength as he thus reflects on his condition, *This home of mine—alas! that I should call this miserable shelter home; it is no abode of luxury and joy, fortune never alighted at my threshold, pleasure makes no stay with me, but want is my constant inmate, and unrelieved affliction is often within these wretched walls. Yes, but in such a home did my Saviour dwell for thirty years; and He, too, endured the privations with which I am so familiar, and submitted to the scorn which mortifies my pride. Shall I then repine? Nay, rather, I will thank Him for the lesson and example which He has set before me, and I will seek for larger supplies of grace, that I may follow with more meekness in His steps, and endure more patiently what He endured.*

'Thus far, however, we have only considered the condition of Christ during his abode at Nazareth. It is now our part to reflect upon his employments there, and we think it possible to derive from such reflections also many valuable practical lessons of almost universal application. And one of them well deserves our close and serious attention. For, perhaps, there are few errors by which we are more commonly misled, than that of regarding the ordinary and humble avocations of life as worthy only of contempt, and as affording no field for the exercise of such virtue as may rightly claim our reverence and praise. The common business of every day, the transient, and, as we think, the trivial occupations of the larger portion of our time, especially if our avocations lie in the humble walks of life; these, if we do not foolishly regard them with contempt, are commonly spoken of as duties which must be got through with, rather than as duties, which, as truly as those we consider higher, require to be well and wisely done.—*The occupations of a general, or a statesman, or a king, have some importance, but how petty and how trivial are my pursuits!*—How frequently does one reflect in this manner on his common occupations! And how naturally do we continue in the same strain: *The higher walks of life; yes, there is some occasion and scope for virtue there, but none in the narrow and secluded path in which I am called, or, I may say, condemned to walk!* Brethren, there are very few of us who do not constantly speak and reason in this manner. . . . . Nevertheless, such thoughts indicate nothing else, except that we are in the habit of taking relative, and not absolute views of the things around us; and, if it were now our purpose, we might adduce satisfactory arguments to prove that the man who helps to build a house, is engaged on a work not less important and essential to the well-being of society than that of the man who is the member of a senate; and that the woman who trains for a community one virtuous child, has done as good service to that community as the general who conducts its wars. But this is not our purpose at this time. We carry your thoughts to higher and more certain ground, and ask, How else can we regard the occupations of this earthly life, however trivial they may seem, except as parts of a vast instrumentality, by which we are to be made ready for our "everlasting habitation." The truth therefore is, that every act we perform is of great and permanent importance; so that we cannot do a trivial thing: the most ordinary deed of the humblest person in this assembly is a deed of highest moment, since it manifests the character of his soul, and is a means whereby that character may be injured or improved. This may be affirmed of all our occupations. And hence it is quite evident that we err in regarding the humble avocations of life as furnishing narrower scope, or fewer occasions for lofty virtue, than the higher. This earthly scene, which is rightly regarded only when it is regarded as a scene of discipline for one of two future worlds, is throughout furnished, and in every department, with means which may be employed in preparation for one or other of those worlds. And if it be true that the soul of every man is of equal value in the sight of God; that He regards not our conventional distinctions of rank, expedient or necessary as they may be to us, but as truly wills the sanctification of a peasant as of a prince; then, it must be also true that He has given to both of these, as His responsible creatures upon earth, equal opportunities of cultivating and maturing that holiness, without which, we are told that, neither of them

I.

can see the Lord. He hath furnished high and ample opportunity of making great moral attainments, of perfecting holiness, in the lowliest as in the loftiest occupations of those whom He will hereafter judge; so that the man of humble life may become as virtuous and as wise as the man who consorts with princes, or controls the affairs of states. Nor can we doubt that heaven will be hereafter peopled with men from all the ranks into which humanity is now divided. Among the glorified saints who will hereafter crowd the streets of the celestial city, and join in the same anthem of ceaseless praise, there will be many who trod on earth the lowliest walks of life, as well as many, we trust, whose paths lay in the highest, and many whose voices upon earth were only heard in the accents of servitude and of submission, as well as many who here spoke only that they might command and be obeyed.

'These lessons, too, on the importance of all the occupations of life, even of the most ordinary and of the humblest, and, on their equal usefulness for the purposes of moral discipline, are surely taught us most impressively by the lowly employments of Our Lord at Nazareth for thirty years. If He had then moved in a higher sphere, or had been engaged in higher duties, our erroneous impressions respecting high spheres and high duties would have been confirmed, and men might then have sighed with more reason for such opportunities as their Lord had chosen. But He took the lowliest paths of life, and occupied Himself with the humblest of its duties; and, in acting thus, He authenticated the reasons we have endeavoured to set forth as opposed to that erroneous impression. If He had been employed for thirty years in the occupations of high rank and office, there would have been some show of reason in our common notion respecting the superior importance of such employments, and the superior opportunities they furnish for high attainments in virtue. But He lived and laboured for that long period as an ordinary mechanic, and He thereby taught us that the occupations of a mechanic, even, are of high importance—of high importance, surely, if the Son of God thought them worthy of His diligent attention for thirty years. He also taught that they may furnish high occasions for the exercise of virtue; and surely this must likewise be admitted, since it was amidst them that He advanced " in favour with God and man," and since the character in which He came forth from His retirement was the most perfect character the world has ever seen.'—*Christ at Nazareth.* Eight Sermons, &c. (Lond. 1845).

By the same Author, 8vo. cloth, 10s. 6d.

THE DIVINE KINGDOM ON EARTH AS IT IS IN HEAVEN.

'Our COMMONWEALTH is in Heaven.'—ST. PAUL.
'Discite in terris cœlestem militiam: hic vivimus, et illic militamus. Cœli mysterium doceat me Deus Ipse, Qui condidit: non homo qui se ipsum ignoravit.'

CONTENTS.

INTRODUCTION.

Importance of realizing the Supernatural Connexions of Man's Existence—How this Realization is effected, and its Results—Erroneous Methods of using the Organs of Revelation for this end—Evil Consequences thence arising—These indicate Objects of men who are taking True Methods—And show the Course which should be adopted by them—Effects flowing from the Efforts thus carried forward—Outline of Plan of the Work which is suggested by these Views.

CHAPTER I.
THE DIVINE ORDER.

Nature of the Divine Order, and its Final Purpose in our View—Called into Existence by the Second Person of the Godhead—Quickening Operations of the Holy Spirit—Typal Form of Created Spiritual Existences—Divine Communications with them—Nature of the Associations which they constitute—Circumstances of their Progress—Helps vouchsafed in it, and its Issues—Failures: Apostasy from the Divine Order—Consequent Conflict of Loyal with Rebellious Spirits—Relations between Various Communities—Apprehension of the Scheme thus carried into Effect—Introduction of Man into the midst of it—Circumstances of his Unfallen State—His Life amidst them, and his Prospects—Forfeiture of those Prospects.

CHAPTER II.

HUMAN APOSTASY: ITS CAUSES AND RESULTS.

Reciprocal Influence and Connexion of Spiritual Existences illustrated—Advantages arising from the Connexion—Its Perversion, and the Consequences—Of Evil Spirits, and their increase of such Perversion—Explanation from this Source of Man's Fall and Loss—Details of Course in which it was effected—Its Consequences shown (1.) In Discord between Man and the Order he was placed in—(2.) In Morbid Reflection of the Mind upon itself—(3.) In Loss of Communion with the Eternal Word—(4.) In Human Discord and Contention—General View of these Evils, and their transmission to Posterity—View of them as Necessary Results from Laws that are Unchangeable—Light in which regarded by Man's Fellow Inheritors of Being—Probability of Occurrence of Similar Events among other Races—Reasons for expecting an Intervention on Man's Behalf—General Account of the Intervention actually effected—Its Main Features, as shown (1.) In Mediator's Nearer Relation with Man—(2.) In His establishment of a Society additional to those originally Constituted—General Review of the Work thus carried forward.

CHAPTER III.

THE RESTORING DISPENSATION: ITS INSTITUTIONS, AND THEIR WORKING.

View of this Dispensation conducts into 'religious' Sphere of Man's Existence—Must be measured by reference to Normal Condition of Being—Nearer Relation of Mediator operates (1.) In Drawing out Introverted Feelings—(2.) In correcting False Views of God—(3.) In re-establishing sense of Law—(4.) In counteracting Divisive Influences of Evil—Recapitulation: General Review of this part of Redeeming Work—Further carried forward by Institution of the Church. Its General Purpose and Design—This carried out (1.) By its Consecration of Times and Places—(2.) By its Institution of Sacrificial Service—(3.) Through the Agency of Representative Priesthood—(4.) By its Aggressive Conflict with the 'World'—(5.) By its Associations for Worship and Service—(6.) Also through Use of its Ordinances as 'Means of Grace'—General Review of Working and Influence of these Institutions—These Purposes carried forward in midst of each Generation on Earth—Also carried forward amidst Departed Generations—Intermediate State (Hades), and its Inhabitants—Of the Knowledge which is conveyed therein—Relation of this State to Man's Condition upon Earth—Consideration of it is necessary to the Completeness of our View of the Church—Views hence suggested as to Communion of its Members—Recapitulation: General View of Church Society—Its complete Adaptation to its Purposes—Fulfilment of Restoring Work. Inferences from its General Aspect and Perfectness—Its Developement in Man's History.

CHAPTER IV.

LAWS OF RESTORING DISPENSATION: THEIR DEVELOPMENT IN HISTORY.

Its Laws Developed by Comparison with it of Man's Proceedings—This Comparison in View of Prophets 'since the World Began'—FIRST RESULT of Comparison seen in Necessity of Trustful Reception of the Remedial Dispensations and

Cordial Use of its Provisions—This necessary for Individual Welfare—It is also necessary for accomplishment of Social Purposes—Completeness of the Revelation for both these Ends—SECOND RESULT of Comparison in showing the purely *instrumental* character of Remedial Institutions—This one of their Fundamental Characteristics—Man's Natural Tendency to overlook it—Effects of this Neglect shown (1.) In State of Heathen World—And (2.) In the Corruptions of the Church—These appear (α), In Intolerance; (β), In Obscured Views of Revealed Disclosures; (γ), In Idolatrous Worship—General View of these Effects—THIRD RESULT of Comparison in showing the Necessity of connecting the 'Supernatural' with the 'Common' Order of Existence—How these were meant to be Combined—Inspired Testimony on this Subject—This confirmed by Consequences of neglecting such Connexion—These Consequences further shown (1.) In Revolt against Spiritual Authority—And (2.) In its Despotic Exercise—Prophetic Protest against both these Evils—FOURTH RESULT of Comparison in bringing out Law of Functional Service—Nature of this Law, and its Universality—It is specially incumbent on Man in his Church Position and Relations—Typal Instances of the Disregard of it in Jewish History—Consequences of neglecting it shown (1.) In Mutual Strife—(2.) In False Views of the Means and Instruments of Grace—(3.) In Neglect of Supernatural Ministrations in the Church—Prophetic Protests against this Neglect—Condemnation of it by Life and Ministry of Unfallen Beings—FIFTH RESULT of Comparison in production of Assurance and Hope—Grounds of such Confidence—History shows (1.) Advantages of holding—(2.) Evils of resigning it—General Review of above Five Laws of Redeeming Dispensation—Growing Neglect of them.

CHAPTER V.
FULFILMENT IN LIFE AND MINISTRY OF CHRIST.

General View of Causes of neglect of above Laws—This neglect reached its Crisis at Period of the Incarnation—Purposes of the Incarnation—Embodiment in Christ, and Manifestation by Him of Divine Order of Man's Being—Shown generally in His habitual Mindfulness of our Supernatural Relations—Then specially (1.) In His exemplary Fulfilment of Family Obligations—(2.) In Heedfulness of Neighbourly Obligations—(3.) In Functional Discharge of Good Works prepared for Him—(4.) In Fulfilment of National Duties and Relationships—(5.) In Observance of Duties and Services of Church Life—This Manifestation of True Order of Human Life made more impressive by 'Signs and Wonders' wrought by Him—Views of Human Conflict with 'Powers of Darkness' thus made known—This Conflict reached its Crisis in His Death—Perfectness of Atoning Sacrifice brought out in that Event—His Ministry in the Intermediate State—Disclosure, in His Resurrection, of Nature of Celestial Beatitude—Recapitulation: Review of His Manifestation of Divine Life—Apostles' Testimony respecting it—Their Declaration of the Laws of Redeeming Dispensation as made known by Him—Recapitulation: Review of their Testimony—Purpose of St. John's Apocalypse. Represents Powers of Evil assailing Divine Kingdom—These seen (1.) in Evils which arise Naturally upon Earth—And then (2.) in Special Chastisements sent Retributively by God—These Evils shown also in course of Diminution and Extinction—Recapitulation: Review of Apocalyptic Visions—Their Purposes in Man's Enlightenment.

CHAPTER VI.
LATER ELUCIDATION AND DEVELOPMENT.

Revelation now perfectly Completed—Causes of Misapprehension of it—Yet everywhere received by Godly Men; and more fully understood by them through Heresies and Unbelief—This illustrated in the cases (1.) of the Judaizers—And (2.) of the Gnostics in the 'Early Church'—Their Errors Reproductions of older Errors and seen again in later—Work of the Fathers with respect to them—Review of Patristic Teaching—Elucidating Work of the Fathers taken up by the Schoolmen—Afterwards by the Mystics and the Systematic Theologians—Services rendered to Godly Men by these Teachers—Their Instruction confirmed by Personal Experience and Historical Events—Extended by instrumentality of Holy Scripture—And by larger Knowledge of Men; also by Scientific Discovery—Recapitulation: Review of these Elucidating Agencies—Results in manifestation of Continuity and Correlation of Man's Existence—Review shows that every Man has been supplied with means of Progress—This also true of every Society—Recapitulation: Results of Elucidating Progress.

CHAPTER VII.
FUTURE PROGRESS AND FULFILMENT.

What thus seen true in Past describes Man's Position now—Institutions of Restoring Dispensation still in Force and Efficacy—Supposition that they were now anywhere accepted—In that place God's Will Embodied; Embodiment must spread—Provincial Communities thus Organized—These must be developed in improved National Life—Relations of Church and Nation in this state—Nations thus raised must be United—Their Mutual Helpfulness in their Union and Intercourse—Their Aggressive Movements on the Dark Places of Earth—Confirmation of such Prospects in 'Prophetical Predictions'—Significance of Restoring Dispensation acknowledged—Man's Earthly Condition approaching that of Intermediate State—This Approach will continue till Close of Earthly Economy—Circumstances of After Life—Possible Future Developments of Divine-Order with reference to Future Destinies of 'Lost'—Closing Meditations.

APPENDIX.

NOTE A.—On the Reasons, supplied by Revelation and interpreted by Science, for believing that there is a community of moral and material nature between ourselves and the inhabitants of other Worlds, and of the light which is hence thrown on Man's Future Life.

NOTE B.—On the Natural Use of Theological Terms and Phrases.

NOTE C.—On the Continuity of the Church.

NOTE D.—Of the True Place of Holy Scripture as part of Divine Revelation, and of the manner in which the Evidences of its Authority should be presented.

NOTE E.—Detailed Application of the Teaching of the Work in the Revival of Church Life; in the Congregation first, then in Ruri-Decanal and Diocesian Synods, and in Convocation—Of the Secular Influences of this Life, and the Method in which Missionary Labours should be carried forward.

Spottiswoode & Co., Printers, New-street Square, London.

LONDON, *June*, 1872.

A CATALOGUE OF BOOKS,

PUBLISHED BY

HENRY S. KING & CO.,

65, CORNHILL.

CONTENTS.

	PAGE
Forthcoming Works	2
German Official Works on the Franco-Prussian War	6
The Cornhill Library of Fiction	7
Forthcoming Novels	8
Recently Published Works	9
Poetry	17
Life and Works of the Rev. F. W. Robertson	19
Sermons by the Rev. Stopford A. Brooke	20
Books on Indian Subjects	21
Recently Published Novels	23
The International Scientific Series	25

65, Cornhill,
June, 1872.

LIST OF BOOKS

PUBLISHED BY

HENRY S. KING & CO.

Forthcoming Works.

I.

A NEW WORK FOR CHILDREN.
THE LITTLE WONDER-HORN.
By JEAN INGELOW.
A Second Series of "Stories told to a Child."
15 Illustrations. Cloth gilt edges, 3s. 6d.
[Immediately.

II.

MEMOIRS OF MRS. LÆTITIA BOOTHBY.
Written by herself in the year 1775.
Edited by WM. CLARK RUSSELL. Author of "The Book of Authors," etc.
Crown 8vo.
[In the press.

III.

THE FORMS OF WATER IN RAIN AND RIVERS, ICE AND GLACIERS.
With 32 Illustrations. By Professor J. TYNDALL, LL.D., F.R.S.
Being Vol. I. of The International Scientific Series.
[In the press.

☞ Prospectuses of the Series may be had of the publishers.
For full announcement of the Series, see the end of this Catalogue.

65, *Cornhill, London.*

IV.
CHANGE OF AIR AND SCENE;
A Physician's Hints about
Doctors, Patients, Hygiène, and Society;
with Notes of Excursions for Health in the Pyrenees, and amongst the Watering-places of France (inland and seaward), Switzerland, Corsica, and the Mediterranean.
From the French of Dr. ALPHONSE DONNÉ.
Large post 8vo.

Utility of Hygiène.—The Hygiène of the Four Seasons.—Exercise and Travels for Health.—Mineral Waters.—Sea Baths.—Hydro-Therapeutics.—Hygiène of the Lungs.—Hygiène of the Teeth.—Hygiène of the Stomach.—Hygiène of the Eyes.—Hygiène of Nervous Women.—The Toilet and Dress.—Notes on Fever. *[Shortly.*

V.
THE HISTORY OF THE CREATION:
Being a Series of Popular Scientific Lectures on the General Theory of Progression of Species; with a Dissertation on the Theories of Darwin, Goethe, and Lamarck; more especially applying them to the Origin of Man, and to other fundamental questions of Natural Science connected therewith.
By Professor ERNST HÆCKEL, of the University of Jena.
With Woodcuts and Plates. *[Shortly.*

VI.
CONTEMPORARY ENGLISH PSYCHOLOGY.
From the French of Professor TH. RIBOT.
An Analysis of the views and opinions of the following Metaphysicians, as expressed in their writings.
James Mill.—A. Bain.—John Stuart Mill.—George H. Lewes.—Herbert Spencer.—Samuel Bailey.
Large post 8vo. *[In the press.*

VII.
PHYSIOLOGY FOR PRACTICAL USE.
By various eminent writers.
Edited by JAMES HINTON,
with 50 Illustrations.

65, *Cornhill, London.*

VIII.
A TREATISE ON RELAPSING FEVER.
By R. T. LYONS,
Assistant-Surgeon, Bengal Army.
Small Post 8vo. [*In the press.*

IX.
BRAVE MEN'S FOOTSTEPS.
A Book of Example and Anecdote for Young People. By the EDITOR of "Men who have Risen."
With Illustrations. Crown 8vo. [*In the press.*

Josiah Wedgwood—the Man of Energy. Granville Sharp—the Negro's earliest Friend. Richard Cobden—the International Man. Dr. William Smith—the Father of English Geology. Andrew Reed—the Stay of the Hopeless. Michael Faraday—the Refined Philosopher. Thomas Wright—the Prison Philanthropist. Joseph Paxton—the Gardener Architect. The Early Life of the late Prince Consort, etc., etc.

X.
THE LIFE AND TIMES OF ROBERT DUDLEY, EARL OF LEICESTER, THE FAMOUS FAVOURITE OF QUEEN ELIZABETH.
From the Private Correspondence of the great Earl of Leicester. By THOMAS WRIGHT, M.A., F.S.A., etc. [*Shortly.*

XI.
CABINET PORTRAITS.
Sketches of Statesmen.
By T. WEMYSS REID.
One Vol., Crown 8vo. [*Shortly.*

Mr. Gladstone.—Mr. Disraeli.—The Earl of Derby.—Mr. Lowe.—Mr. Hardy.—Mr. Bright.—Earl Granville.—Lord Cairns.—Marquis of Hartington.—Mr. Wilson-Patten.—The Earl of Carnarvon.—Earl Russell.—Lord John Manners.—Mr. Cardwell.—Lord Hatherley.—Mr. Henley.—The Duke of Argyll.—Sir Stafford Northcote.—Earl Grey.—The Marquis of Salisbury.—The Duke of Richmond.—Lord Westbury.—Mr. Forster.—Mr. Newdegate.—Sir Roundell Palmer.—Lord Lytton.—The Late Earl of Derby.—Late Earl of Clarendon.

65, *Cornhill, London.*

XII.
BOKHARA: ITS HISTORY AND CONQUEST.
By Professor ARMINIUS VAMBERY, of the University of Pesth
Author of "Travels in Central Asia," etc.

Two vols., demy 8vo.   [*In the press.*

XIII.
BRIEFS AND PAPERS.
Being Sketches of the Bar and the Press.
By Two Idle Apprentices.

Crown 8vo.   [*Shortly.*

Our Leading Columns.—Our Special Correspondent.—Our Own Reporter.—In the Gallery.—Our Special Wire.—The Story of the Fogborough Englishman.—In the Temple.—Westminster Hall.—On Circuit.—Scissors and Paste.—A Rising Junior.—Country Sessions.—An Eminent Leader.—Lincoln's Inn.—At the Old Bailey.

XIV.
SOLDIERING AND SCRIBBLING.
By ARCHIBALD FORBES, of the *Daily News*, Author of "My Experience of the War between France and Germany."

A Penny a Day.—The Christmas Cattle Market.—Soldiers' Wives.—The Story of the Megæra.—In a Military Prison.—German War Prayers.—Flogged.—Sunday Afternoon at Guy's.—Butcher Jack's Story.—Bummarees.—A Deserter's Story.—Lions and Lion-Tamers.—Our March on Brighton.—Catsmeat.—Army Crimes and Punishments.—Whisky.—Furs.—Some Christmases.

XV.
HOME-WORDS FOR WANDERERS.
Sermons by ARTHUR S. THOMPSON, B.D.,
British Chaplain at St. Petersburg.

IMPORTANT GERMAN OFFICIAL WORKS ON THE FRANCO-PRUSSIAN WAR.

I.
THE OPERATIONS OF THE GERMAN ARMIES IN FRANCE, FROM SEDAN TO THE END OF THE WAR OF 1870–1. With large Official Map. From the Journals of the Head-Quarters Staff. By Major WILLIAM BLUME. Translated by E. M. JONES, Captain 20th Foot, late Professor of Military History, Sandhurst. Demy 8vo, Price 9s. [*Just out.*

II.
TACTICAL DEDUCTIONS FROM THE WAR OF 1870–1. By Capt. A. V. BOGUSLAWSKI. Translated by Col. LUMLEY GRAHAM, Late 18th (Royal Irish) Regiment. Demy 8vo. Uniform with the above. Price 7s. [*Just out.*

"Above all should every infantry officer make these tactical conclusions the object of his serious studies, about which there must be great controversy. Out of these deductions alone can we get the lessons in infantry operations for war, and for training during peace. In all essential things, according to our conviction, the author has rightly apprehended the lessons of the late war, and his views are a guide and criterion that will be of service to every officer."—*Militair Wochenblatt.*

III.
THE OPERATIONS OF THE SOUTH ARMY IN JANUARY AND FEBRUARY, 1871. By COUNT WARTENSLEBEN, of the Prussian General Staff. Translated by Colonel WRIGHT. Demy 8vo. Uniform with the above. [*Just out.*

IV.
STUDIES IN TROOP-MARCHING. By Col. VON VERDY DU VERNOIS. Translated by Lieut. H. J. T. HILDYARD, 71st Foot. Demy 8vo. Uniform with the above. [*Parts I. and II. are in the press.*

V.
THE ARMY OF THE NORTH-GERMAN CONFEDERATION. A brief description of its organization, of the different branches of the Service and their *rôle* in war, of its mode of fighting, etc. By a Prussian General. Translated from the German by Col. EDWARD NEWDIGATE. Demy 8vo. Uniform with the above. [*In the press.*

65, Cornhill, London.

The Cornhill Library of Fiction.

It is intended in this Series to produce books of such merit that readers will care to preserve them on their shelves. They are well printed on good paper, handsomely bound, with a Frontispiece, and are sold at the moderate price of 3s. 6d. each.

I.
ROBIN GRAY. By CHARLES GIBBON. With a Frontispiece by Hennessy. [*Ready.*

II.
KITTY. By Miss M. BETHAM-EDWARDS. [*Ready.*

III.
HIRELL. By JOHN SAUNDERS, Author of "Abel Drake's Wife." [*Ready.*

IV.
ABEL DRAKE'S WIFE. By JOHN SAUNDERS, Author of "Hirell." [*Shortly.*

V.
FOR LACK OF GOLD. By CHARLES GIBBON, Author of "Robin Gray."

VI.
ONE OF TWO. By J. HAIN FRISWELL, Author of "The Gentle Life," etc.

VII.
GOD'S PROVIDENCE HOUSE. By Mrs. G. LINNÆUS BANKS.

VIII.
THE HOUSE OF RABY. By Mrs. HOOPER.

Other Standard Novels to follow.

PANDURANG HARI.
A Tale of Mahratta Life, sixty years ago.
Edited, from the edition of 1826.
By Sir HENRY BARTLE E. FRERE, G.C.S.I., K.C.B.
[*Shortly.*

AN ARABIC AND ENGLISH DICTIONARY OF THE KORAN.
By Major J. PENRICE. Post 4to. [*In the press.*

MEMOIRS OF VILLIERSTOWN.
By C. S. J. Crown 8vo. With Frontispiece.
[*In the press.*

65, *Cornhill, London.*

FORTHCOMING NOVELS.

I.
HONOR BLAKE; THE STORY OF A PLAIN WOMAN. By Mrs. KEATINGE, Author of "English Homes in India." Two vols., crown 8vo. [*Nearly ready.*

II.
THE DOCTOR'S DILEMMA. By HESBA STRETTON, Author of "Little Meg," etc., etc.

III.
HESTER MORLEY'S PROMISE. By HESBA STRETTON, Author of "Little Meg," "Alone in London," "David Lloyd's Will." Three vols., crown 8vo. [*In the press.*

IV.
ISRAEL MORT, OVERMAN. THE STORY OF THE MINE. By JOHN SAUNDERS, Author of "Hirell," "Abel Drake's Wife," etc. Three vols., crown 8vo. [*In the press.*

V.
A NEW STORY. By ALICE FISHER, Author of "Too Bright to Last." Three vols., crown 8vo.

VI.
THE SPINSTERS OF BLATCHINGTON. By MAR. TRAVERS. 2 vols.

VII.
A NEW WORK. By Col. MEADOWS TAYLOR, Author of "Tara," etc. In three vols.

VIII.
A LITTLE WORLD. By GEO. MANVILLE FENN, Author of "The Sapphire Cross," "Mad," etc.

IX.
THE HIGH MILLS. By KATHERINE SAUNDERS, Author of "Gideon's Rock," "The Haunted Crust," etc.

65, Cornhill, London.

FORTHCOMING NOVELS—(continued).

X.
OFF THE SKELLIGS. By JEAN INGELOW. In three vols.

XI.
WHAT 'TIS TO LOVE. By the Author of "Flora Adair," "The Value of Fosterstown," etc.

XII.
THROUGH LIFE. By Mrs. NEWMAN. One vol., crown 8vo.

XIII.
LISETTE'S VENTURE. By Mrs. RUSSELL GRAY. Two vols., crown 8vo.

Recently Published Works.

I.
SEPTIMIUS. A Romance. By NATHANIEL HAWTHORNE. Author of "The Scarlet Letter," "Transformation," etc. One Volume, crown 8vo. Cloth extra, gilt, 9s.

A peculiar interest attaches to this work. It was the last thing the author wrote, and he may be said to have died as he finished it.

II.
MEMOIRS OF LEONORA CHRISTINA, Daughter of Christian IV. of Denmark. Written during her imprisonment in the Blue Tower of the Royal Palace at Copenhagen, 1663-1685. Translated by F. E. BUNNETT (*Translator of Grimm's "Life of Michael Angelo," &c.*) With a beautiful Autotype Portrait of the Countess. Medium 8vo.

III.
LIVES OF ENGLISH POPULAR LEADERS. No. 1. Stephen Langton. By C. EDMUND MAURICE. Crown 8vo.

65, *Cornhill, London.*

IV.
STREAMS FROM HIDDEN SOURCES. By B. Montgomerie Ranking. Crown 8vo.

THE SEVEN STREAMS ARE:

Cupid and Psyche.
The Life of St. Eustace.
Alexander and Lodowick.
Sir Urre of Hungary.
Isabella; or, The Pot of Basil.
The Marriage of Belphegor.
Fulgencius.

"Out of all old lore I have chosen seven books as setting forth seven following stages of time, and from each of these have taken what seemed to me the best thing, so that any man may judge, and if it please him trace it to its source."—*Extract from Preface.*

V.
THE ENGLISH CONSTITUTION. By Walter Bagehot. A New Edition, revised and corrected, with an Introductory Dissertation on recent changes and events. Crown 8vo, 7s. 6d.

CONTENTS.—The Cabinet.—The Pre-requisites of Cabinet Government, and the Peculiar Form which they have assumed in England.—The Monarchy.—The Monarchy (*continued*).—The House of Lords.—The House of Commons.—On Changes of Ministry.—Its supposed Checks and Balances.—Its History, and the Effects of that History.—Conclusion.—Appendix.

VI.
THOUGHTS FOR THE TIMES. By the Rev. H. R. Haweis, M.A., Author of "Music and Morals," etc. Crown 8vo. 6s.

INTRODUCTORY.—I. The Liberal Clergy. GOD.—II. Conception. III. Experience. CHRISTIANITY.—IV. Character. V. History. THE BIBLE.—VI. Essence. VII. Doctrine. THE ARTICLES.—VIII. The Trinity. Original Sin. IX. Predestination. The Church. LIFE.—X. Pleasure. XI. Sacrifice. WORSHIP.—XII. The Lord's Day. XIII. Preaching. CONCLUSION.—XIV. The Law of Progress.

VII.
SIX PRIVY COUNCIL JUDGMENTS—1850-1872. Annotated by W. G. Brooke, M.A., Barrister-at-Law. Cr. 8vo.

1. Gorham *v.* Bishop of Exeter.—2. Westerton *v.* Liddell.—3. Williams *v.* Bishop of Salisbury, and Wilson *v.* Fendal.—4. Martin *v.* Mackonochie.—5. Hibbert *v.* Purchas.—6. Sheppard *v.* Bennett.

VIII.
HERMANN AGHA: An Eastern Narrative. By W. GIFFORD PALGRAVE, Author of "Travels in Central Arabia," etc. 2 vols., Crown 8vo. Cloth, extra gilt, 18s.

IX.
ALEXIS DE TOCQUEVILLE. Correspondence and Conversations with NASSAU W. SENIOR, from 1833 to 1859. Edited by Mrs. M. C. M. SIMPSON. Two Vols., Large Post 8vo. 21s.

X.
From the Author's latest Stereotyped Edition,
MISS YOUMANS' FIRST BOOK OF BOTANY. Designed to cultivate the observing powers of children. New and Enlarged Edition, with 300 Engravings. Crown 8vo, 5s.

XI.
AN ESSAY ON THE CULTURE OF THE OBSERVING POWERS OF CHILDREN, Especially in connection with the Study of Botany. By ELIZA A. YOUMANS, of New York. Edited, with Notes and a Supplement on the Extension of the Principle to Elementary Intellectual Training in General, by JOSEPH PAYNE, Fellow of the College of Preceptors: Author of "Lectures on the Science and Art of Education," etc. Crown 8vo. 2s. 6d.

XII.
OVER VOLCANOES; OR, THROUGH FRANCE AND SPAIN IN 1871. By A. KINGSMAN. Crown 8vo.

"The writer's tone is so pleasant, his language is so good, and his spirits are so fresh, buoyant, and exhilarating, that you find yourself inveigled into reading, for the thousand-and-first time, a description of a Spanish bull-fight."—*Illustrated London News.*

"The adventures of our tourists are related with a good deal of pleasantry and humourous dash, which make the narrative agreeable reading."—*Public Opinion.*

"A work which we cordially recommend to such readers as desire to know something of Spain as she is to-day. Indeed, so fresh and original is it, that we could have wished that it had been a bigger book than it is."—*Literary World.*

65, *Cornhill, London.*

* *

XIII.

IN QUEST OF COOLIES. A South Sea Sketch. By JAMES L. A. HOPE. Crown 8vo, with 15 Illustrations from Sketches by the Author. Price 6s. Second Edition.

[*Just out.*

"At the present moment, when considerable attention has been directed to the South Seas, by the murder of Bishop Patteson, the little book before us arrives most opportunely. . . . Mr. Hope's description of the natives is graphic and amusing, and the book is altogether well worthy of perusal."—*Standard.*

" Lively and clever sketches."—*Athenæum.*

" This agreeably written and amusingly illustrated volume."—*Public Opinion.*

XIV.

ROUND THE WORLD IN 1870. A Volume of Travels, with Maps. By A. D. CARLISLE, B.A., Trin. Coll., Camb. Demy 8vo, 16s.

" Makes one understand how going round the world is to be done in the quickest and pleasantest manner, and how the brightest and most cheerful of travellers did it with eyes wide open and keen attention all on the alert, with ready sympathies, with the happiest facility of hitting upon the most interesting features of nature and the most interesting characteristics of man, and all for its own sake."—*Spectator.*

" Delightfully written, as unpretentious and as entertaining a sketch of travel as we have seen for a long time."—*Scotsman.*

" We can only commend, which we do very heartily, an eminently sensible and readable book."—*British Quarterly Review.*

XV.

THE NILE WITHOUT A DRAGOMAN. (Second Edition.) By FREDERIC EDEN. In one vol., crown 8vo, cloth, 7s. 6d.

"Should any of our readers care to imitate Mr. Eden's example, and wish to see things with their own eyes, and shift for themselves, next winter in Upper Egypt, they will find this book a very agreeable guide."—*Times.*

"Gives, within moderate compass, a suggestive description of the charms, curiosities, dangers, and discomforts of the Nile voyage."—*Saturday Review.*

" We have in these pages the most minute description of life as it appeared on the banks of the Nile; all that could be seen or was worth seeing in nature or in art is here pleasantly and graphically set down. . . . It is a book to read during an autumn holiday."—*Spectator.*

XVI.

SCRIPTURE LANDS IN CONNECTION WITH THEIR HISTORY. By G. S. DREW, M.A., Rector of Avington, Winchester, Author of "Reasons of Faith." Second Edition. Bevelled boards, 8vo, price 10s. 6d.

"Mr. Drew has invented a new method of illustrating Scripture history—from observation of the countries. Instead of narrating his travels and referring from time to time to the facts of sacred history belonging to the different countries, he writes an outline history of the Hebrew nation from Abraham downwards, with special reference to the various points in which the geography illustrates the history. The advantages of this plan are obvious. Mr. Drew thus gives us not a mere imitation of 'Sinai and Palestine,' but a view of the same subject from the other side . . . He is very successful in picturing to his readers the scenes before his own mind. The position of Abraham in Palestine is portrayed, both socially and geographically, with great vigour. Mr. Drew has given an admirable account of the Hebrew sojourn in Egypt, and has done much to popularize the newly-acquired knowledge of Assyria in connection with the two Jewish kingdoms. We look with satisfaction to the prospect of a larger work from the same author, and are confident that he cannot adopt a method better suited to his talents and knowledge, or more generally useful in the present state of Biblical literature."—*Saturday Review.*

"This volume will be read by every Biblical student with equal profit and interest. We do not remember any work in which the Scripture has been interwoven so admirably with the natural history of the places in which its transactions happened. It has been written in a devout and reverential spirit, and reflects great credit on its author as a man of learning and a Christian. We regard it has a very seasonable contribution to our religious literature."—*Record.*

XVII.

ECHOES OF A FAMOUS YEAR. By HARRIET PARR Author of "The Life of Jeanne d'Arc," "In the Silver Age,' etc. Crown 8vo, 8s. 6d.

"A graceful and touching, as well as truthful account of the Franco-Prussian War. Those who are in the habit of reading books to children will find this at once instructive and delightful."—*Public Opinion.*

"Miss Parr has the great gift of charming simplicity of style: and if children are not interested in her book, many of their seniors will be."—*British Quarterly Review.*

65, *Cornhill, London.*

XVIII.
JOURNALS KEPT IN FRANCE AND ITALY, FROM 1848 TO 1852.
With a Sketch of the Revolution of 1848. By the late NASSAU WILLIAM SENIOR. Edited by his daughter, M. C. M. SIMPSON. In two vols., post 8vo, 24s.

"The present volume gives us conversations with some of the most prominent men in the political history of France and Italy . . . as well as with others whose names are not so familiar or are hidden under initials. Mr. Senior has the art of inspiring all men with frankness, and of persuading them to put themselves unreservedly in his hands without fear of private circulation."—*Athenæum.*

"The book has a genuine historical value."—*Saturday Review.*

"No better, more honest, and more readable view of the state of political society during the existence of the second Republic could well be looked for."—*Examiner.*

"Of the value of these volumes as an additional chapter in the history of France at the period when the Republic passed into the Empire, it is impossible to speak too highly."—*Public Opinion.*

XIX.
THE SECRET OF LONG LIFE.
Dedicated by special permission to LORD ST. LEONARDS. Large crown 8vo, 5s.

"A pleasantly written volume, of a very suggestive character."—*Standard.*

"Some shrewd observations, illustrated by references to a number of remarkable instances of long life."—*Public Opinion.*

"A very pleasant little book, which is always, whether it deal in paradox or earnest, cheerful, genial, scholarly."—*Spectator.*

"The bold and striking character of the whole conception is entitled to the warmest admiration."—*Pall Mall Gazette.*

"We should recommend our readers to get this book . . . because they will be amused by the jovial miscellaneous and cultured gossip with which he strews his pages."—*British Quarterly Review.*

XX.
JEAN JAROUSSEAU, THE PASTOR OF THE DESERT.
From the French of EUGÈNE PELLETAN. Translated by Colonel E. P. DE L'HOSTE. In fcap. 8vo, with an engraved frontispiece, price 5s.

"There is a poetical simplicity and picturesqueness; the noblest heroism; unpretentious religion.; pure love, and the spectacle of a household brought up in the fear of the Lord.. . . . The whole story has an air of quaint antiquity similar to that which invests with a charm more easily felt than described the site of some splendid ruin."—*Illustrated London News.*

"This charming specimen of Eugène Pelletan's tender grace, humour, and high-toned morality."—*Notes and Queries.*

"A touching record of the struggles in the cause of religious liberty of a real man."—*Graphic.*

XXI.

THE SUBSTANTIVE SENIORITY ARMY LIST. First Issue. Majors and Captains. Containing the Names of all Substantive Majors and Captains, Serving upon Full-pay or Retired upon Half-pay, arranged according to their Seniority in the Service, and in such order as immediately to exhibit the standing of every such Major or Captain for Promotion in his own Arm of the Service, whether Cavalry, Artillery, Engineers, Infantry, or Marines, specifying their particular Corps, and distinguishing those holding Higher Brevet-rank. By Captain F. B. P. WHITE, 1st W. I. Regiment. 8vo, sewed, 2s. 6d.

XXII.

DISCIPLINE AND DRILL. Four Lectures delivered to the London Scottish Rifle Volunteers. By Captain S. FLOOD PAGE, Adjutant of the Regiment, late 105th Light Infantry, and Adjutant of the Edinburgh Rifle Brigade. Just published. A Cheaper Edition, price 1s.

"One of the best-known and coolest-headed of the metropolitan regiments, whose adjutant moreover has lately published an admirable collection of lectures addressed by him to the men of his corps."—*Times*.

"Capt. Page has something to say . . . . and in every case it is said moderately, tersely, and well."—*Daily Telegraph*.

"The very useful and interesting work. . . . Every Volunteer, officer or private, will be the better for perusing and digesting the plain-spoken truths which Captain Page so firmly, and yet so modestly, puts before them; and we trust that the little book in which they are contained will find its way into all parts of Great Britain."—*Volunteer Service Gazette*.

"The matter . . . is eminently practical, and the style intelligible and unostentatious."—*Glasgow Volunteer News*.

XXIII.

CATHOLICISM AND THE VATICAN. With a Narrative of the Old Catholic Congress at Munich. By J. LOWRY WHITTLE, A.M., Trin. Coll., Dublin. Crown 8vo, 4s. 6d.
[*Just out.*

"We cannot follow the author through his graphic and lucid sketch of the Catholic movement in Germany and of the Munich Congress, at which he was present; but we may cordially recommend his book to all who wish to follow the course of the movement."—*Saturday Review*.

"A valuable and philosophic contribution to the solution of one of the greatest questions of this stirring age."—*Church Times*.

65, *Cornhill, London.*

XXIV.

NAZARETH: ITS LIFE AND LESSONS. In small 8vo, cloth, 5s. By the Author of "The Divine Kingdom on Earth as it is in Heaven." [*Just out.*

"*In Him was life, and the life was the light of men.*"

"A singularly reverent and beautiful book; the style in which it is written is not less chaste and attractive than its subject."—*Daily Telegraph.*

"We would earnestly commend it for attentive perusal to those who are proposing to undertake, or have just entered upon, the sacred ministry in our church."—*Morning Post.*

"Perhaps one of the most remarkable books recently issued in the whole range of English theology. . . . Original in design, calm and appreciative in language, noble and elevated in style, this book, we venture to think, will live."—*Churchman's Magazine.*

XXV.

THE DIVINE KINGDOM ON EARTH AS IT IS IN HEAVEN. In demy 8vo, bound in cloth. Price 10s. 6d. "Our COMMONWEALTH is in Heaven." [*Now ready.*

"It is seldom that, in the course of our critical duties, we have to deal with a volume of any size or pretension so entirely valuable and satisfactory as this. Published anonymously as it is, there is no living divine to whom the authorship would not be a credit . . . Not the least of its merits is the perfect simplicity and clearness, conjoined wit a certain massive beauty, of its style."—*Literary Churchman.*

"A high purpose and a devout spirit characterize this work. It is thoughtful and eloquent . . . The most valuable and suggestive chapter is entitled 'Fulfilment in Life and Ministry of Christ,' which is full of original thinking admirably expressed."—*British Quarterly Review.*

POETRY.

I.
SONGS OF LIFE AND DEATH. By JOHN PAYNE, Author of "Intaglios," "Sonnets," "The Masque of Shadows," etc. Cr. 8vo, 5s. [*Just out.*

II.
SONGS OF TWO WORLDS. By a NEW WRITER. Fcap. 8vo, cloth, 5s.

"The 'New Writer' is certainly no tyro. No one after reading the first two poems, almost perfect in rhythm and all the graceful reserve of true lyrical strength, can doubt that this book is the result of lengthened thought and assiduous training in poetical form. . . . These poems will assuredly take high rank among the class to which they belong."—*British Quarterly Review, April 1st.*

"No extracts could do justice to the exquisite tones, the felicitous phrasing and delicately wrought harmonies of some of these poems."—*Nonconformist, March 27th.*

"Are we in this book making the acquaintance of a fine and original poet, or of a most artistic imitator? And our deliberate opinion is that the former hypothesis is the right one. It has a purity and delicacy of feeling like morning air."—*Graphic, March 16th.*

"If these poems are the mere preludes of a mind growing in power and in inclination for verse, we have in them the promise of a fine poet. . . . The verse describing Socrates has the highest note of critical poetry."—*Spectator, Feb. 17th.*

"One of the most promising of the books of verse by new writers which have appeared for a considerable time. Very little is wanted in the more artistic of these poems."—*Civil Service Gazette, March 9th.*

"The author is a real poet."—*Public Opinion, Feb. 17th.*

"Many of the songs exhibit exquisite fancy and considerable imaginative power. . . . We should have been glad to make further quotations from these admirable poems."—*Manchester Examiner, Feb. 8th.*

"The writer possesses, and has by much cultivation enhanced, the gift which is essential to lyrical poetry of the highest order."—*Manchester Guardian, Jan. 11th.*

"So healthy in sentiment and manly in tone that one cannot help feeling an interest in the writer."—*Examiner Dec. 30th.*

"The 'New Writer' is a thoroughly accomplished master of versification,—his thought is clear and incisive, his faculty of expression and power of ornamentation ought to raise him to a high rank among the poets of the day."—*Glasgow Herald, Dec. 28th.*

65, Cornhill, London.

III.
THE LEGENDS OF ST. PATRICK, AND OTHER POEMS.
By AUBREY DE VERE. Crown 8vo, 5s. [*Just out.*

IV
EROS AGONISTES. By E. B. D. Crown 8vo, 3s. 6d.
[*Just out.*

V
THE INN OF STRANGE MEETINGS, AND OTHER POEMS. By MORTIMER COLLINS. Crown 8vo, 5s.

"Mr. Collins has an undercurrent of chivalry and romance beneath the trifling vein of good humoured banter which is the special characteristic of his verse. . . . The 'Inn of Strange Meetings' is a sprightly piece."—*Athenæum.*

"Abounding in quiet humour, in bright fancy, in sweetness and melody of expression, and, at times, in the tenderest touches of pathos."—*Graphic.*

VI.
ASPROMONTE, AND OTHER POEMS. Second Edition, cloth, 4s. 6d.

"The volume is anonymous; but there is no reason for the author to be ashamed of it. The 'Poems of Italy' are evidently inspired by genuine enthusiasm in the cause espoused; and one of them, 'The Execution of Felice Orsini,' has much poetic merit, the event celebrated being told with dramatic force."—*Athenæum.*

"The verse is fluent and free."—*Spectator.*

VII.
THE DREAM AND THE DEED, AND OTHER POEMS.
By PATRICK SCOTT, Author of "Footpaths Between Two Worlds," etc. Fcap. 8vo, cloth, 5s.

"A bitter and able satire on the vices and follies of the day, literary, social, and political."—*Standard.*

"Shows real poetic power coupled with evidences of satirical energy."—*Edinburgh Daily Review.*

65, *Cornhill, London.*

Life and Works

of the

Rev. Fred. W. Robertson.

NEW AND CHEAPER EDITIONS.

LIFE AND LETTERS OF THE LATE REV. FRED. W. ROBERTSON, M.A. Edited by STOPFORD BROOKE, M.A., Hon. Chaplain in Ordinary to the Queen. Library Edition, in demy 8vo, with Steel Portrait. 12s.

A Popular Edition, in one vol., is now ready,
Price 6s.

SERMONS :—Price 3s. 6d. per vol.

First Series	Small crown 8vo.
Second Series . . .	Small crown 8vo.
Third Series	Small crown 8vo.
Fourth Series . . .	Small crown 8vo.

EXPOSITORY LECTURES ON ST. PAUL'S EPISTLE TO THE CORINTHIANS. Small crown 8vo. 5s.

LECTURES AND ADDRESSES ON LITERARY AND SOCIAL TOPICS. Small crown 8vo. 3s. 6d.

AN ANALYSIS OF MR. TENNYSON'S "IN MEMORIAM." (Dedicated by permission to the Poet-Laureate.) Fcap. 8vo. 2s.

THE EDUCATION OF THE HUMAN RACE. Translated from the German of GOTTHOLD EPHRAIM LESSING. Fcap. 8vo. 2s. 6d.

A LECTURE ON FRED. W. ROBERTSON, M.A. By the Rev. F. A. NOBLE, delivered before the Young Men's Christian Association of Pittsburgh, U.S. 1s. 6d.

65, Cornhill, London.

SERMONS BY THE REV. STOPFORD A. BROOKE, M.A.
Honorary Chaplain to Her Majesty the Queen.

I.
THE LIFE AND WORK OF FREDERICK DENISON MAURICE. A Memorial Sermon. Crown 8vo, sewed. 1s.

II.
CHRIST IN MODERN LIFE. Sermons preached in St. James's Chapel, York Street, London. Second Edition. Crown 8vo. 7s. 6d.

"Nobly fearless and singularly strong . . . carries our admiration throughout."—*British Quarterly Review.*

III.
FREEDOM IN THE CHURCH OF ENGLAND. Second Edition. Six Sermons suggested by the Voysey Judgment. In One Volume. Crown 8vo, cloth, 3s. 6d.

"Every one should read them. No one can be insensible to the charm of his style, or the clear logical manner in which he treats his subject."—*Churchman's Monthly.*

"We have to thank Mr. Brooke for a very clear and courageous exposition of theological views, with which we are for the most part in full sympathy."—*Spectator.*

"Interesting and readable, and characterized by great clearness of thought, frankness of statement, and moderation of tone."—*Church Opinion.*

"A very fair statement of the views in respect to freedom of thought held by the liberal party in the Church of England."—*Blackwood's Magazine.*

IV.
SERMONS PREACHED IN ST. JAMES'S CHAPEL, YORK STREET, LONDON. Fifth Edition. Crown 8vo. 6s.

"No one who reads these sermons will wonder that Mr. Brooke is a great power in London, that his chapel is thronged, and his followers large and enthusiastic. They are fiery, energetic, impetuous sermons, rich with the treasures of a cultivated imagination."—*Guardian.*

"Mr. Brooke's sermons are shrewd and clever, and always readable. He is better off than many preachers, for he has something to say, and says it."—*Churchman's Magazine.*

"A fine specimen of the best preaching of the Episcopal pulpit."—*British Quarterly.*

65, Cornhill, London.

BOOKS ON INDIAN SUBJECTS.

I.

THE EUROPEAN IN INDIA. A Hand-book of practical information for those proceeding to, or residing in, the East Indies, relating to Outfits, Routes, Time for Departure, Indian Climate, etc. By EDMUND C. P. HULL. With a MEDICAL GUIDE FOR ANGLO-INDIANS. Being a compendium of Advice to Europeans in India, relating to the Preservation and Regulation of Health. By R. S. MAIR, M.D., F.R.C.S.E., late Deputy Coroner of Madras. In one vol., post 8vo, 6s.

"Full of all sorts of useful information to the English settler or traveller in India."—*Standard.*

"One of the most valuable books ever published in India—valuable for its sound information, its careful array of pertinent facts, and its sterling common sense. It is a publisher's as well as an author's 'hit,' for it supplies a want which few persons may have discovered, but which everybody will at once recognise when once the contents of the book have been mastered. The medical part of the work is invaluable."—*Calcutta Guardian.*

II.

EASTERN EXPERIENCES. By L. BOWRING, C.S.I., Lord Canning's Private Secretary, and for many years the Chief Commissioner of Mysore and Coorg. In one vol., demy 8vo, 16s. Illustrated with Maps and Diagrams.

"An admirable and exhaustive geographical, political, and industrial survey."—*Athenæum.*

"The usefulness of this compact and methodical summary of the most authentic information relating to countries whose welfare is intimately connected with our own, should obtain for Mr. Lewin Bowring's work a good place among treatises of its kind."—*Daily News.*

"Interesting even to the general reader, but more especially so to those who may have a special concern in that portion of our Indian Empire."—*Post.*

"An elaborately got up and carefully compiled work."—*Home News.*

III.

A MEMOIR OF THE INDIAN SURVEYS. By CLEMENT R. MARKHAM. Printed by order of Her Majesty's Secretary of State for India in Council. Imperial 8vo, 10s.

65, *Cornhill, London.*

BOOKS ON INDIAN SUBJECTS—*(continued)*.

IV.

WESTERN INDIA BEFORE AND DURING THE MUTINIES. Pictures drawn from Life. By Major-General Sir GEORGE LE GRAND JACOB, K.C.S.I., C.B. In one vol., crown 8vo, 7s. 6d.

"The most important contribution to the history of Western India during the Mutinies, which has yet, in a popular form, been made public."—*Athenæum.*

"The legacy of a wise veteran, intent on the benefit of his countrymen rather than on the acquisition of fame."—*London and China Express.*

"Few men more competent than himself to speak authoritatively concerning Indian affairs."—*Standard.*

V.

EXCHANGE TABLES OF STERLING AND INDIAN RUPEE CURRENCY, upon a new and extended system, embracing values from one farthing to one hundred thousand pounds, and at rates progressing, in sixteenths of a penny, from 1s. 9d. to 2s. 3d. per rupee. By DONALD FRASER, Accountant to the British Indian Steam Navigation Co., Limited. Royal 8vo, 10s. 6d.

VI.

A CATALOGUE OF MAPS OF THE BRITISH POSSESSIONS IN INDIA AND OTHER PARTS OF ASIA. Published by Order of Her Majesty's Secretary of State for India in Council. Royal 8vo, sewed, 1s.

A continuation of the above, sewed, price 6d., is now ready.

☞ *Messrs. Henry S. King & Co. are the authorised agents by the Government for the sale of the whole of the Maps enumerated in this Catalogue.*

VII.

THE BENGAL QUARTERLY ARMY LIST.			Sewed, 15s.
THE BOMBAY	DO.	DO.	Sewed, 9s.
THE MADRAS	DO.	DO.	Sewed, 12s.

65, Cornhill, London.

Recently Published Novels.

I.
THE PRINCESS CLARICE. A STORY OF 1871. By MORTIMER COLLINS. Two vols., crown 8vo. [*Just Out.*

II.
A GOOD MATCH. By AMELIA PERRIER. Author of "Mea Culpa." Two vols. [*Just out.*
"Racy and lively."—*Athenæum.*
"Agreeably written."—*Public Opinion.*

III.
THOMASINA. By the author of "Dorothy," "De Cressy," etc. Two vols., crown 8vo. [*Just out.*
"We would liken it to a finished and delicate cabinet picture, in which there is no brilliant colour, and yet all is harmony; in which no line is without its purpose, but all contribute to the unity of the work."—*Athenæum.*
"For the delicacies of character-drawing, for play of incident, and for finish of style, we must refer our readers to the story itself: from the perusal of which they cannot fail to derive both interest and amusement."—*Daily News.*
"Very pleasant and lively reading."—*Graphic.*
"This undeniably pleasing story."—*Pall Mall Gazette.*

IV.
THE STORY OF SIR EDWARD'S WIFE. By HAMILTON MARSHALL, Author of "For Very Life." One vol., crown 8vo. [*Just out.*
"There are many clever conceits in it . . . Mr. Hamilton Marshall proves in 'Sir Edward's Wife' that he can tell a story closely and pleasantly."—*Pall Mall Gazette.*
"A quiet graceful little story."—*Spectator.*
"There is a freshness and vigour in Mr. Marshall's writings that will be enjoyed by the thoughtful reader."—*Public Opinion.*

V.
LINKED AT LAST. By F. E. BUNNETT. One vol, crown 8vo.
"'Linked at Last' contains so much of pretty description, natural incident, and delicate portraiture, that the reader who once takes it up will not be inclined to relinquish it without concluding the volume."—*Morning Post.*
"A very charming story."—*John Bull.*
"A very simple and beautiful story."—*Public Opinion.*

65, *Cornhill, London.*

VI.

PERPLEXITY. By SYDNEY MOSTYN, a New Writer. Three vols., crown 8vo. [*Just out.*

"Unquestionably a very powerful story. What may be called its manipulation is exceedingly able, inasmuch as it is told in an autobiographical form; and yet it exhibits the thoughts, feelings, ideas, and temptations of a woman of varied and interesting characteristics."—*Morning Post.*

"We congratulate Sydney Mostyn on the production of a deeply interesting work, full of manly thoughts, admirable reflections, and sparkling humour. The work is aptly named, and we can assure its author we shall experience no perplexity when others from his pen lie on our table."—*Public Opinion.*

"Shows much lucidity, much power of portraiture, and no inconsiderable sense of humour."—*Examiner.*

"The literary workmanship is good, and the story forcibly and graphically told."—*Daily News.*

"Written with very considerable power, the plot is original and . . . worked out with great cleverness and sustained interest."—*Standard.*

VII.

CRUEL AS THE GRAVE. By the COUNTESS VON BOTHMER. Three vols., crown 8vo.

"*Jealousy is cruel as the Grave.*"

"The Wise Man's motto is prefixed to an interesting, though somewhat tragic story, by the Countess von Bothmer. . . . Her German prince, with his chivalrous affection, his disinterested patriotism, and his soldierlike sense of duty, is no unworthy type of a national character which has lately given the world many instances of old-fashioned heroism."—*Athenæum.*

"This graceful story—tender and gay, with the sweetest tenderness and the brightest gaiety,—whether pathetic or satirical, is always natural and never dull."—*Morning Post.*

"An agreeable, unaffected, and eminently readable novel."—*Daily News.*

VIII.

HER 'TITLE OF HONOUR. By HOLME LEE. One vol., crown 8vo. (Second Edition.)

"It is unnecessary to recommend tales of Holme Lee's, for they are well known, and all more or less liked. But this book far exceeds even our favourites, *Sylvan Holt's Daughter*, *Kathie Brande*, and *Thorney Hall*, because with the interest of a pathetic story is united the value of a definite and high purpose."—*Spectator.*

"We need scarcely say of a book of Holme Lee's writing, that it is carefully finished and redolent of a refined and beautiful soul. We have no more accomplished or conscientious literary artist."--*British Quarterly.*

"A most exquisitely written story."—*Literary Churchman.*

65, Cornhill, London.

65, CORNHILL,
June, 1872.

THE
INTERNATIONAL SCIENTIFIC SERIES.

——oo°⚬°oo——

MESSRS. HENRY S. KING & Co. have the pleasure to announce that under the above title they intend to issue a SERIES of POPULAR TREATISES, embodying the results of the latest investigations in the various departments of Science at present most prominently before the world.

The character and scope of the Series will be best indicated by a reference to the names and subjects included in the following List ; from which it will be seen that the co-operation of many of the most distinguished Professors in England, America, Germany, and France has been already secured.

Although these Works are not specially designed for the instruction of beginners, still, as they are intended to address the *non-scientific public*, they will be, as far as possible, explanatory in character, and free from technicalities. The object of each author will be to bring his subject as near as he can to the general reader.

The Series will also be published simultaneously in New York by Messrs. D. Appleton & Co. ; in Paris by M. Germer Baillière ; and in Leipzig by Messrs. Brockhaus. The volumes will be crown 8vo size, well printed on good paper, strongly and elegantly bound, and will sell in this country at a price *not exceeding Five Shillings.*

A first List of Authors and Subjects is appended ; but several of the titles are provisional. The first volume, by Professor **JNO. TYNDALL**, F.R.S., entitled "**THE FORMS OF WATER IN RAIN AND RIVERS, ICE AND GLACIERS**," is now in the Press, and will be *published in the Autumn.* It is impossible at present to give a definite announcement of the order of publication ; but it is expected that besides Professor Tyndall's book the following will be issued during the present year :—

THE PRINCIPLES OF MENTAL PHYSIOLOGY. By Dr. CARPENTER.

BODILY MOTION AND CONSCIOUSNESS. By Professor HUXLEY, F.R.S.

PHYSICS AND POLITICS. By WALTER BAGEHOT.

FOOD AND DIETS. By Dr. EDWARD SMITH, F.R.S.; and

EARTH-SCULPTURES. By Professor RAMSAY, F.R.S.

INTERNATIONAL SCIENTIFIC SERIES—FIRST LIST.

Professor T. H. HUXLEY, LL.D., F.R.S.
 BODILY MOTION AND CONSCIOUSNESS.
Dr. W. B. CARPENTER, LL.D., F.R.S.
 THE PRINCIPLES OF MENTAL PHYSIOLOGY.
Sir JOHN LUBBOCK, Bart., F.R.S.
 THE ANTIQUITY OF MAN.
Professor RUDOLPH VIRCHOW (of the University of Berlin).
 MORBID PHYSIOLOGICAL ACTION.
Professor ALEXANDER BAIN, LL.D.
 RELATIONS OF MIND AND BODY.
Professor BALFOUR STEWART, LL.D., F.R.S.
 THE CONSERVATION OF ENERGY.
WALTER BAGEHOT, Esq.
 PHYSICS AND POLITICS.
Dr. H. CHARLTON BASTIAN, M.D., F.R.S.
 THE BRAIN AS AN ORGAN OF MIND.
HERBERT SPENCER, Esq.
 THE STUDY OF SOCIOLOGY.
Professor WILLIAM ODLING, F.R.S.
 THE NEW CHEMISTRY.
Professor W. THISELTON DYER, B.A., B.Sc.
 FORM AND HABIT IN FLOWERING PLANTS.
Dr. EDWARD SMITH, F.R.S.
 FOOD.
Professor W. KINGDON CLIFFORD, M.A.
 THE FIRST PRINCIPLES OF THE EXACT SCIENCES EXPLAINED TO THE NON-MATHEMATICAL.
Mr. J. N. LOCKYER, F.R.S.
 SPECTRUM ANALYSIS.
W. LAUDER LINDSAY, M.D., F.R.S.E.
 MIND IN THE LOWER ANIMALS.
Dr. J. B. PETTIGREW, M.D., F.R.S.
 WALKING, SWIMMING, AND FLYING.
Professor A. C. RAMSAY, LL.D., F.R.S.
 EARTH SCULPTURE: Hills, Valleys, Mountains, Plains, Rivers, Lakes; how they were Produced, and how they have been Destroyed.

INTERNATIONAL SCIENTIFIC SERIES—FIRST LIST.

Professor JOHN TYNDALL, LL.D., F.R.S.
THE FORMS OF WATER IN RAIN AND RIVERS, ICE AND GLACIERS.

Dr. HENRY MAUDSLEY.
RESPONSIBILITY IN DISEASE.

Professor W. STANLEY JEVONS.
THE LOGIC OF STATISTICS.

Professor MICHAEL FOSTER, M.D.
PROTOPLASM AND THE CELL THEORY.

Rev. M. J. BERKELEY, M.A., F.L.S.
FUNGI: their Nature, Influences, and Uses.

Professor CLAUDE BERNARD (of the College of France).
PHYSICAL AND METAPHYSICAL PHENOMENA OF LIFE.

Professor A. QUETELET (of the Brussels Academy of (Sciences). SOCIAL PHYSICS.

Professor H. SAINTE CLAIRE DEVILLE.
AN INTRODUCTION TO GENERAL CHEMISTRY.

Professor WURTZ.
ATOMS AND THE ATOMIC THEORY.

Professor D. QUATREFAGES.
THE NEGRO RACES.

Professor LACAZE-DUTHIERS.
ZOOLOGY SINCE CUVIER.

Professor BERTHELOT.
CHEMICAL SYNTHESIS.

Professor J. ROSENTHAL (of the University of Berlin).
(Subject not yet received).

Professor JAMES D. DANA, M.A., LL.D.
On CEPHALIZATION; or, Head-Characters in the Gradation and Progress of Life.

Professor S. W. JOHNSON, M.A.
ON THE NUTRITION OF PLANTS.

Professor AUSTIN FLINT, Jr., M.D.
THE NERVOUS SYSTEM AND ITS RELATION TO THE BODILY FUNCTIONS.

Professor W. D. WHITNEY.
MODERN LINGUISTIC SCIENCE.

PLEASURE:

A HOLIDAY BOOK OF PROSE AND VERSE.

Illustrated. Elegantly Bound in Ornamental Cloth Cover with Gilt Edges and Illuminated Frontispiece, 2s. 6d. Illuminated Cover, sewed, 1s.

CONTENTS.

The Miserable Family	Hain Friswell.
Sleep by the Sea. A Poem	Tom Hood.
The New Pass	Amelia B. Edwards.
A Regret. A Poem	The Hon. Mrs. Norton.
The Echo of the Bells	Alice Fisher.
The Critical Spirit	Rev. Canon Kingsley.
A Scene on Olympus	Percival Keane.
Tristram and Iseult. A Poem	Algernon C. Swinburne.
How Bayard Married his old Love	Holme Lee.
After Some Years	Laura Leigh.
Love and Revenge	Countess Von Bothmer.
Time: an Apologue	Thomas Purnell.
A Tale of High Colour. A Poem	Godfrey Turner.
A New Lease of Life	Thomas Archer.
The Gambling Hands	The Hon. Mrs. Norton.

"An extraordinary shilling's worth. 'Tristram and Iseult' is alone worth far more than the price of the publication, which is a very good annual, and very creditable both to the editor and publisher."—*Standard*.

Monthly, Price One Shilling.

THE MINING MAGAZINE AND REVIEW.

A
RECORD OF MINING, SMELTING, QUARRYING, AND ENGINEERING.

Edited by **NELSON BOYD**, *F.G.S., Etc.*

HENRY S. KING & CO., 65, CORNHILL, LONDON.

www.ingramcontent.com/pod-product-compliance
Lightning Source LLC
Chambersburg PA
CBHW030819190426
43197CB00036B/617